HUMAN
BODY

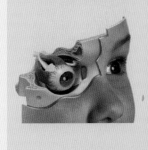

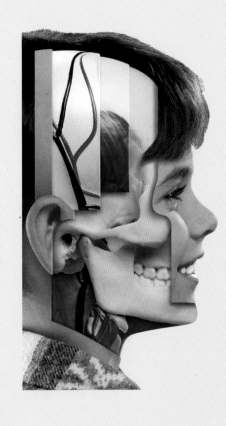

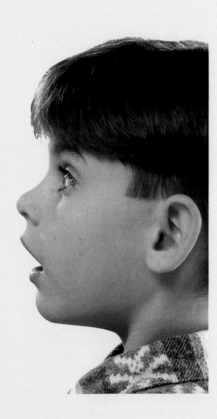

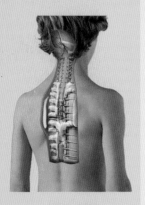

THIS IS A CARLTON/WATTS BOOK

Text and design copyright © Carlton Books Limited 1996
Special photography and image manipulation © Carlton Books Limited 1996

10 9 8 7 6 5 4 3 2 1

First published in 1996 by Franklin Watts
96 Leonard Street London EC2A 4RH

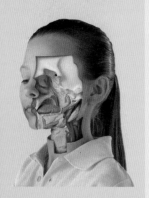

A CIP catalogue record for this book is available from the British Library

ISBN 0-7496-2538-4

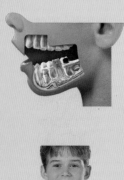

Project art director: Russell Porter
Special photography: Matthew Ward
Quantel operator: Sunil Chhatralia
Project editor: Liz Wheeler
Editor: Kate Swainson
Picture research: Charlotte Bush
Production: Garry Lewis

Anatomical models supplied by:
Educational + Scientific Products Limited, England
Paul Binhold, Germany

Image manipulation produced on Quantel Printbox™
Colour reproduction by Colourpath, London

Printed and bound in Dubai

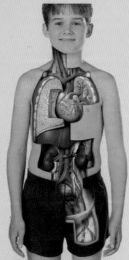

HUMAN BODY

An inside look at you

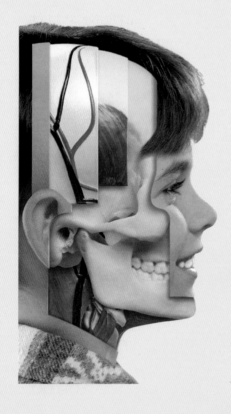

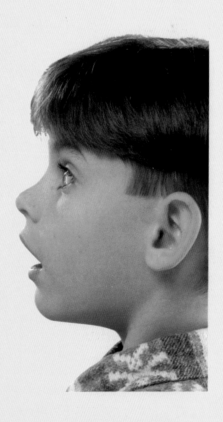

STEVE PARKER

Consultant Editor **DR TIM WOOTTON**

W

FRANKLIN WATTS

LONDON • NEW YORK • SYDNEY

contents

5

the senses 84

7

reproduction 110

6

communication and control 98

introduction

We marvel at the complex machines and sophisticated devices of our modern world. We are Space-aged, Technology-obsessed, Information-rich and Computer-crazy. Yet the most wonderful machine in the known Universe is right here with you now. You may spend so much time gazing out of it at the TV screen, the roadway or the classroom wall that you rarely pause to look inward, to see how this incredible device works.

A *biological machine*

Of course, this machine is the human body. Its basic design has been around for many thousands of years, although your own personal version is probably much younger! How does the body compare with the latest hi-tech computerized devices that seem to be swamping our surroundings and daily lives?

The human body is not a mechanical device, but a biological one. Its structure and functions are endlessly intricate. It is made of dozens of large parts called

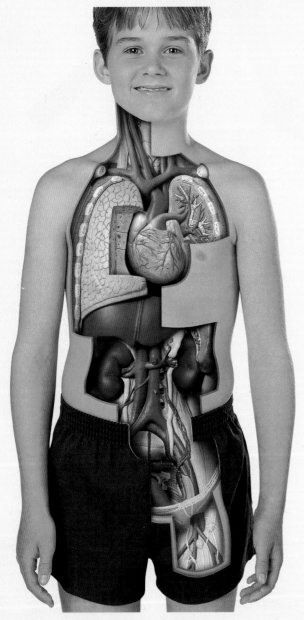

The main body, or torso, contains dozens of different organs.

organs, each with their own tasks to perform. The organs are made from hundreds of tissues, which are formed from billions of microscopic cells that do thousands of jobs. All these parts work together for the whole being. However, they are wrapped up in a flexible covering of skin, so we rarely get the chance to peek inside.

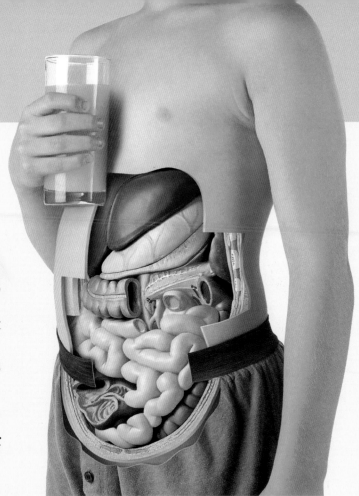

The lower torso, or abdomen, is the ultimate food processor.

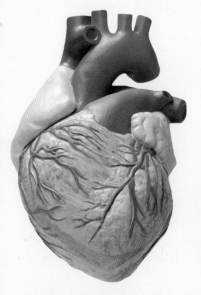

No mechanical pump can match the heart's efficiency and longevity.

A *living machine*

The human machine has all the hallmarks of animal life here on Earth. It can live, breathe, move and feed. It is a social creature, communicating with its fellow humans by a vast variety of sounds, signs and gestures, and the squiggles of words and pictures. Its physical body grows and develops largely by itself, according to a pre-determined plan or "blueprint" which we call its genes. The many parts maintain, mend and repair themselves for dozens of years, far outlasting most mechanical devices. And human bodies can make more human bodies similar to themselves, by the process of breeding or reproduction.

Continued overleaf

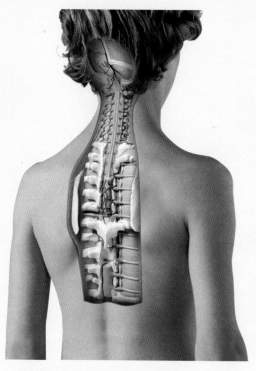

The backbone, or spine, is the body's central supporting girder, strong yet flexible.

A *thinking machine*

Perhaps most marvellous of all, the human body is a thinking machine. It has awareness and consciousness, thoughts and feelings, wishes and wants, memories and emotions. It can learn, make decisions, create ideas, and experience pleasure and pain. All these events take place inside its control centre – the coconut-sized, wrinkled, greyish lump inside its head, the brain.

A *questioning machine*

This book looks at the human body in many different ways, using research and information from the latest generations of microscopes, scanners and computerized medical equipment. Why is the body the shape and

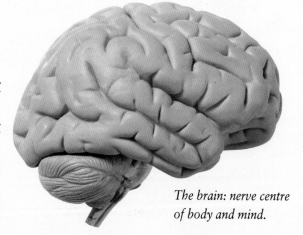

The brain: nerve centre of body and mind.

size that it is? What are its main design features, and why? What is under the skin? How do the many different parts work? What happens to the air, food and drink that go into the body? What comes back out in return? How does the body grow and develop from its pinhead-sized beginnings? And how is this incredible device managed and controlled? The answers to our own questions about our own bodies will fascinate every one of us.

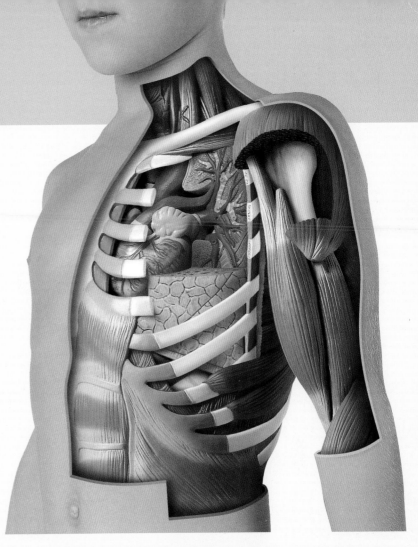

The pictures in this book

The unique images in *Human Body* have been produced using the latest computer paintbox techniques. These have manipulated and combined photographs of real, living people with photographs of accurate anatomical models.

The models show the body's inner parts, from large organs such as

Layer by deeper layer, computer-based impositions combine seven images (four shown below) into one revealing cutaway view.

the heart and liver, down to microscopic cells and their own inner parts. The computerized painting and image-enhancement methods allow us to "see into" real bodies in clear, accurate and fascinating three-dimensional detail. And all without spilling one drop of blood!

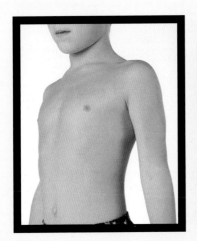
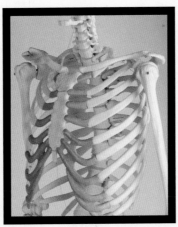
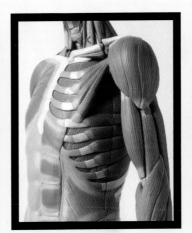
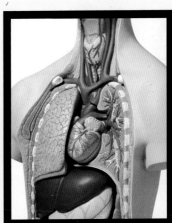

chapter

1

shape and structure

THE NEXT TIME you gaze into a mirror, take time out for a few seconds. Imagine that you are a space alien, seeing the human body for the first time. What are its main features? Most of the body is covered with skin. There are openings here and there, such as the eyes, ears, nostrils and mouth, as well as those lower down. There are two long arms and two even longer, stronger legs, joined to a central portion called the torso. Most of the sensing areas, which see, hear, taste and smell, are gathered in the large upper lump, which has a furry top. These are known as the head and the hair.

When you look around, you see lots of other human bodies. They are different colours, from almost white to pink, light brown, darker brown and almost black. Some are tall while others are shorter, and some are wide while others are narrower. This is partly because some bodies are old while others are younger. The body grows and changes through its life. Yet we are all humans, made of the same basic ingredients. If the space alien could peer through the skin, it would see that inside we are all much the same.

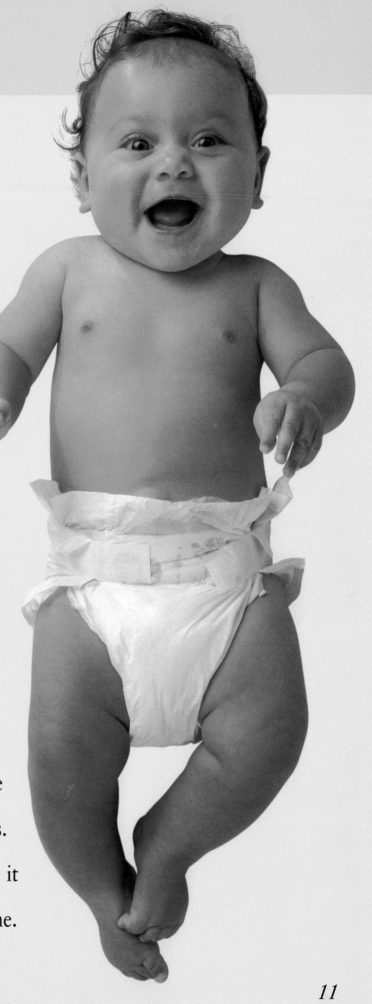

basic body features

THE MAIN FEATURES OF THE HUMAN BODY are so obvious that we rarely think about them. Of course we have two eyes, two ears, two arms and two legs. But why? Many animals have four or six legs, some ten or more. There are animals with six eyes, others with antennae (feelers) on their heads, and many with tails. The answers to why we look like we do go back millions of years – into our evolutionary past. Most scientists accept that humans – like all other living things from germs to fungi, oak trees to giraffes – have come about by the process of evolution. This involves gradual change over many generations, over extremely long periods of time. The human body has been shaped by evolution to fit the needs of nature, such as moving about, finding and eating food, escaping from enemies, and surviving in the wild.

global family

We are used to picking out individuals in a crowd. We recognize slight differences in facial features, eye colour, hair styles and clothes. But these small variations are overwhelmed by the overall similarities in body shape and design, such as two arms, two legs and one head. Imagine if these varied as much as hair styles!

Vertebrates and mammals

Humans belong to the major group of animals called vertebrates. These include fish, reptiles, amphibians, birds and mammals. They all have an inner supporting skeleton, usually of bones, including a main backbone. One side of a vertebrate's skeleton is a mirror-image of the other, which scientists call bilateral symmetry. This is why our bodies are organized on a two-sided body plan rather than a circular one (radial symmetry) like a starfish.

Within the vertebrates, we are in the group called mammals. All mammals have warm blood and fur or hair. Mother mammals feed their babies on milk from special glands on the mother's body, called mammary glands. Most mammals have four limbs. Humans have all of these features; this explains why we are mammals.

The human king of the apes

Among the mammals, we belong to the group called primates. This includes lemurs, monkeys and apes. They have a generally upright body position, two large forward-facing eyes, and long-fingered hands that can grasp. We have these body features too. Our closest cousins are the great apes – chimps, gorillas and orang-utans. The apes lost their tails during evolution.

The human body's overall shape is very familiar. We see it in the mirror every day. This familiarity makes it easy to forget that it has evolved over millions of years.

Human bodies span the globe. No other large creature on Earth has evolved so successfully or is so widespread.

This is why we are tail-less. Just as well, or putting on jeans would be very awkward.

Slow change

About 5–10 million years ago, our prehistoric ancestors probably looked similar to chimpanzees today. Gradually, they evolved into humans. The story is told by fossilized bones and teeth dug from the rocks, in Africa, Asia and Europe. The body became taller and more upright, so that it walked on two legs. The "front legs" became arms, for holding and manipulating. The brain and upper head increased in size, but the face and jaws became smaller in proportion. The thick body hairs gradually shrank. By 100,000 years ago, the human had evolved. Carrying in its body the signs of its past – vertebrate, mammal, primate and ape – it was spreading across the world.

the range of mammals

These creatures look very different but they are all mammals. They have the essential features of a backbone, warm blood, fur or hair, and milk-producing mammary glands in the female to make food for the babies. During millions of years of evolution, some of these features have disappeared or changed. A dolphin's skin is almost perfectly smooth, with hardly any hair. The kangaroo has fur, but the female gives birth at an early stage of her young's development, and carries it around in a pouch. The armadillo's fur is covered by its armour of bony plates. Inside, they are still mammals.

size and shape

O F ALL THE PEOPLE YOU KNOW, who has the smallest body? Some adults are shorter than others. But babies are far smaller than any adults. There are two main reasons why the body varies in height. One is age. As we get older, so we grow taller. Growth does not happen at a constant rate. It is fastest before birth, in the womb. Young babies also get bigger rapidly, then their growth begins to slow down. It speeds up again during the teenage years. By about 18–20 years of age, most people have reached their full adult height, and growth stops. The body may get smaller in later years.

The other main reason for height differences comes from our genes. The genes are the "body's blueprint", a complicated set of instructions for building and operating a human body. (Genes are described in more detail on page 122.) A baby inherits two sets of genes, one from each parent. These genes control every body process, including growth, and so have a great effect on final adult height. The way that genes are passed on means that tall parents are likely to have tall children and shorter parents produce shorter children. But this is not always the case, and many variations occur.

(Genes are described in more detail on page 122.)

changing shape

As a body grows from baby to adult, its proportions change. Compared to the overall height, the head gets smaller while the limbs, especially the legs, become longer. You can see this clearly in this selection of body photographs, adjusted so that the bodies all have the same height.

Fat and muscle – a weighty issue

Size is also width and weight. The genes control whether a body has large bones, and this usually produces features such as wide shoulders and hips, or a deep chest. However, a person's body outline and shape can be affected much more by what's inside – fat and muscle. Eat too much, and fat builds up. This gives flabby bulges, especially in the abdomen (belly), buttocks and hips. Do lots of activity and exercise, and muscles become bigger and stronger. This makes the body bulge where the muscles are just under the skin, such as in the shoulders and upper chest, upper arms, thighs and calves. You cannot do

face to face

When we look at other human bodies, we usually concentrate on the face. Facial features help us to recognize people and their facial expressions show if they are happy or sad, friendly or angry. Our features are largely inherited, under control of the genes, and this is why we resemble our parents. Skin colour is also partly inherited and partly affected by exposure to sunlight (see page 26).

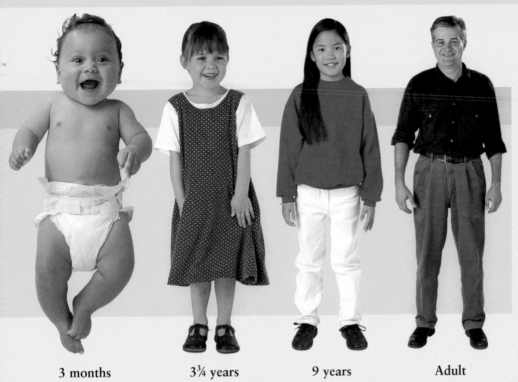

| 3 months | 3¾ years | 9 years | Adult |

much to change your height, but you can do lots to affect your body outline, width, shape and weight.

Sex differences

Another essential feature that affects the body's overall size and shape is its sex – whether the person is male or female. There is little difference between boys and girls up to the age of nine or ten years. But toward adulthood, men usually become taller and heavier than women. They generally have a more angular body outline, with wider shoulders. Women tend to have a more rounded body outline, with wider hips.

But we should remember that there is enormous variation in the size, shape and colour of the human body. For example, there are millions of women who are taller than men. Improved health and food in some countries has meant that children in those countries today, are up to five centimetres taller than children of the same age would have been fifty years ago. The range of what is "normal" is very wide. This endless variation is what makes the body so fascinating!

body chemistry

The body must stay warm, otherwise its chemistry cannot work.

EVERYTHING IN THE UNIVERSE, from a grain of sand to a giant star, is made of atoms. There are untold billions of atoms – over 100 billion billion in a drop of water! But there are only about 100 different kinds of atom. These are called the basic chemical substances, or elements. They include hydrogen, oxygen, iron, sulphur and chlorine.

The human body is no exception. It, too, is made of chemical elements. If you could use a very sensitive machine to analyse a human body in a chemical laboratory, you would detect more than 20 different elements as its main ingredients. About $^{99}/_{100}$ths of the body consists of just six elements. These are oxygen, carbon, hydrogen, nitrogen, calcium and phosphorus. The other elements in a human body are called trace elements, which means that they are present in tiny amounts.

Mixing molecules and elements to the right recipe

If you combine elements into molecules, the molecules have properties different from the separate elements. For example, hydrogen and oxygen are normally invisible gases. Add two atoms of hydrogen to one atom of oxygen, and you have H_2O – water, a clear liquid. In fact, much of the body's oxygen and hydrogen are combined in this way, as water. It means that, by weight, you are two-thirds water. For an average adult, this is 37 litres of water. Next time you visit the supermarket or shop, try to imagine 37 one-litre bottles of mineral water. It makes a very wet body!

These elements and molecules do not drift about at random. If they did, the body would be a muddy chemical soup of ingredients, each floating about on its own. The key to the human body, like any object, is the way that these chemical ingredients, the elements and molecules, are combined. Some of these molecules are small, like the sugars in your blood which give you energy. Others are huge, with hundreds of thousands of atoms, like the proteins which make up your skin, muscles and bones. But even these giant molecules are too small to see. In fact, even the most powerful microscopes can only just make them out. Only when millions of these giant molecules are joined together in specific arrangements can we see them with our own eyes, and recognize them as a flake of skin or piece of hair.

rich and poor

Most people in rich countries have no problem getting the new chemicals they need for their bodies. They can choose from many kinds of food, and eat the right amounts to stay healthy. But too much of certain foods is not a good thing, since eating too much of the wrong kind of food brings its own problems, such as heart disease. People from poor countries usually have less choice, and may be unable to eat enough to keep healthy. Sadly, many simply have too little food to stay alive.

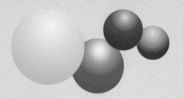

Renewing the elements

The same chemicals do not remain inside the body for ever. There is a constant coming and going of atoms and molecules as the body moves, grows and repairs itself, and gets rid of old waste. Fresh supplies of chemicals come from food.

The speed of turnover differs for various elements. Some stay in the body for years, like the minerals calcium and phosphorus which make your bones strong. Others have been and gone in a few days, like the sodium and potassium needed for healthy nerves. Indeed, measuring the amount and turnover of body chemicals is an important part of medicine. It can show if a disease is present. There are many sensitive laboratory tests that medical scientists can perform. These measure hundreds of different substances in the blood, urine and other body parts and products. Sometimes, replacing the chemicals with better foods or medicines can cure the disease.

body ingredients

Chemical element	Proportion of total weight (%)	Grams in average adult body
OXYGEN	65	39,000
CARBON	18.5	11,100
HYDROGEN	9.5	5,700
NITROGEN	3.2	1,920
CALCIUM	1.5	900
PHOSPHORUS	1	600
POTASSIUM	0.4	240
SULPHUR	0.3	180
CHLORINE	0.2	120
SODIUM	0.2	120
MAGNESIUM	0.1	60

Other main elements:
Iodine, iron, cobalt, copper, fluorine, manganese, zinc, silicon

Tiniest traces:
Vanadium, chromium, selenium

smaller and smaller

AS THE JETLINER TAXIS OUT to the runway for take-off, its engines begin to cough and splutter. Warning lights flash, and it returns to the hangar. But what's the problem? A modern jumbo jet has four million different components! The experienced engineer first checks the main systems, such as the electrics, hydraulics and fuel. If the problem is electrical, the next task is to identify the main part at fault, such as a generator or fuse. Working in this way, the problem is identified, the plane is soon mended, checked and on its way.

The human body is much more complicated than any machine. But it is organized in a similar way, and this helps us to understand how it works. The whole body is made up of about 12 major systems. These include the digestive system which deals with food, the circulatory system which pumps blood around, the sensory system which detects what goes on around the body, and the muscular system which produces body movements. These systems are described in each chapter throughout this book.

Each body system is made up of main parts working together. In the digestive system, for instance, these are the mouth and teeth, gullet, stomach and intestines. The major parts are called organs. Each organ is made of tissues, and in turn, each tissue is made of cells. The cells are the microscopic building blocks of the body. Tissues and cells are shown in detail on page 21.

inside facts

➤ The body's largest organs are the skin on the outside and the liver on the inside.

➤ The smallest organs include tiny touch sensors in the skin and tiny lymph nodes, smaller than pinheads, which protect you from invaders and disease (see pages 80–81).

➤ The most important organ is the brain, the place where we think, and what makes us human. Many other organs are not essential for life, and some can be replaced by machine versions for a time – even the heart and kidneys.

Look inside

How do we know all this? From ancient times, surgeons cut open people while trying to treat and cure them. Medical scientists also dissected dead bodies (and sometimes live ones), to see what was inside and how the body worked. Our understanding increased in the seventeenth century, with the invention of the microscope. For the first time, people could see the miniature world of cells and how they grew, moved, multiplied, died and were replaced by new cells. They could also see invaders and how these harmed the body. Today we can look into the living body, without pain or harm. Doctors use a range of medical scanners and imagers which "see" inside the body, without making any cuts at all. These machines use various kinds of wave, such as radio, X-ray and sound, as well as special cameras and computers to produce a picture of the organs and tissues under the skin. There are also pictures of entire "cyberbodies" stored in computer memories. Using the methods of modern electronics and virtual reality, you can look into them from any direction and angle.

see inside

Most of what you see on the outside of the body is its biggest organ – the skin. Peel this away by the magic of computer graphics, and beneath are muscles, the basic organs of the muscular system which powers our movements. Running through and between the muscles are parts of two body-wide systems – the thread-like nerves of the nervous system and the blood-carrying tubes or vessels of the circulatory system. Go deeper still and you reveal the bones of the skeletal system, which gives the whole body strength and support. The main bones shown here are the ribs.

Continue inwards into the chest and you reach the lungs, chief organs of the respiratory system for getting oxygen into the body. Nestling between the two lungs is the heart, the ever-beating muscular pump of the circulatory system. The body is like this all the way through, with organs and other parts compactly squashed against each other. There are no empty holes or wasted space.

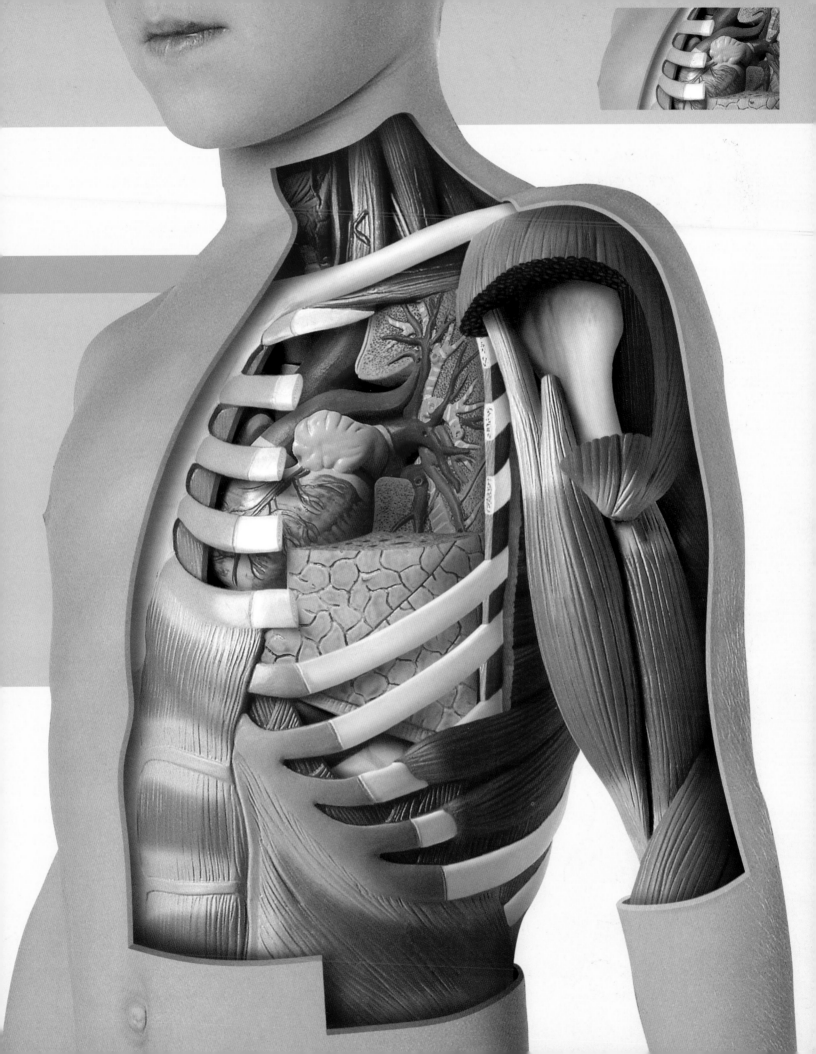

body building blocks

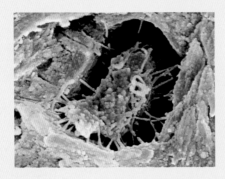

This is a bone cell, or osteocyte. It builds hard bone around itself.

ALL LIVING THINGS, plant and animal, are made from cells. Some are just a single cell, like the bag-of-jelly amoeba oozing across the mud of a pond. The human body is made of more than 50 billion billion cells. An individual body cell is too small to be seen with the unaided eye. Only with the invention of the light microscope, nearly 400 years ago, could people study the world of the very tiny, and make out that cells were the basic ingredients of all life. In the human body, most cells are 10–50 micrometres (µm) across. On average, this means about 40 cells in a line would stretch one millimetre. However, the line would be only one cell wide and far too thin to see! Cells are mostly water and almost transparent. Only when they are grouped in millions can we see them.

Cells in different shapes and sizes

Body cells come in hundreds of shapes and sizes, depending on where they are, and the jobs they do. The largest cell in the body is the egg cell or ovum, which may be fertilized by a sperm cell and grow into a baby. A ripe egg cell is about 100 micrometres across. Among the smallest cells are doughnut-shaped red blood cells, only 7 micrometres across.

Body cells are grouped with cells of their same kind, as tissues. Lots of muscle cells make muscle tissue. Stacks of skin cells form skin, and so on. Different tissues make up the body's organs. The organs work together as systems. And the systems function with each other to make up the body.

inside a cell

This is a typical cell. It is not exactly the same as any particular cell in the body, but it shows all the main features of a cell. Many body cells have completely different shapes, some being long and thin, while some are wide and flat.

The complex structure of cells

Things do not float about at random inside a cell. Every cell is highly organized. It has a complicated set of inner structures based on sheet-like membranes. In the same way that the body is made of major parts called organs, the parts of a cell are called organelles. Just like walls and floors divide a building into rooms, membranes divide the cell into hundreds of different compartments and chambers.

The membrane on the outside is like an outer skin. Inside there are dozens more membranes forming the organelles. Some are spread out, folded and stacked in piles. Others are coiled and twisted to form the room-like compartments. Still others form shapes like balls, balloons and sausages which contain stores of useful chemicals or waste for disposal. Cell chemicals pass through "doors" in the membranes between organelles. They also pass through holes or pores in the main cell membrane, into and out of the whole cell.

These are fat, or adipose, cells. They are used for storing energy and food.

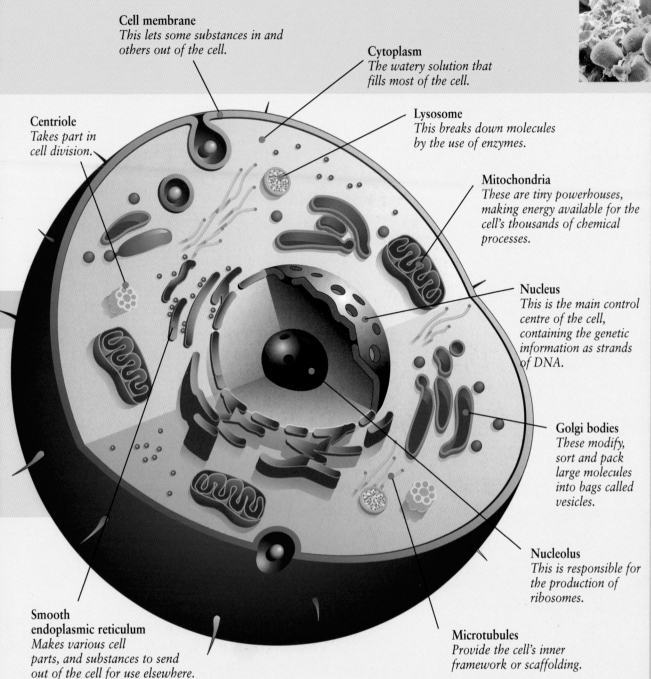

Cell membrane
This lets some substances in and others out of the cell.

Cytoplasm
The watery solution that fills most of the cell.

Lysosome
This breaks down molecules by the use of enzymes.

Centriole
Takes part in cell division.

Mitochondria
These are tiny powerhouses, making energy available for the cell's thousands of chemical processes.

Nucleus
This is the main control centre of the cell, containing the genetic information as strands of DNA.

Golgi bodies
These modify, sort and pack large molecules into bags called vesicles.

Nucleolus
This is responsible for the production of ribosomes.

Microtubules
Provide the cell's inner framework or scaffolding.

Smooth endoplasmic reticulum
Makes various cell parts, and substances to send out of the cell for use elsewhere.

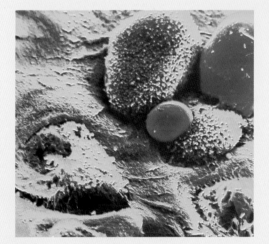

These cartilage cells, or chondrocytes, make stiff hoops of cartilage in the windpipe.

Inner strength and control

Even the watery-looking parts of the cell, called the cytoplasm, are not empty. They contain microtubules and microfilaments, which are the cell's inner "scaffolding". They give strength and shape. In some cells they also get longer or shorter, so that the cell can change shape and ooze along like a micro-slug.

The cell's control centre, the nucleus contains all the information and instructions to keep the cell alive and functioning. The information the cell needs is in the form of immensely long coils of chemicals. These are known as DNA, which make up the genes.

how cells grow

CELLS DO NOT LAST FOR EVER. Like the body they are in, they are born, they live and they die. This is a natural part of body growth, maintenance and repair. Even the atoms, molecules and other parts of an individual cell are changed gradually during the life of that cell. Imagine a house that is maintained by changing a brick here, and a window or roof tile there a little at a time over the years. After a long period, there are no original parts left. The body is similar. You probably have very few molecules still in your body that were there when you were born! Most cells survive for much shorter periods than the whole body. Their life spans are programmed into the genetic instructions. Some are dead and gone within a few hours. This happens especially at places where the body has a lot of physical wear and tear, such as the skin, and inside the mouth, stomach and intestines.

If cells are continuously wearing out and rubbing away and dying, where do new cells come from? They are made by cell division (which is also known as cell multiplication!). Put simply, one cell splits down the middle into two. Each half has its own cell membrane and its share of organelles and other parts. The two offspring cells grow back to the size of the parent cell. Then they split, too. And so on.

Copying genes from mother and father

An important part of cell division involves the nucleus. Each nucleus contains two sets of genes. One came originally from the person's father, and one from the mother. If one set went into each offspring cell, then how could the offspring cell divide properly? One of its own offspring cells would have no genes at all. So, before a cell divides, both sets of genes are copied. This is termed DNA replication. Each offspring cell then receives a full double-set of genes, one from the father and one from the mother. In this way, all the cells in the body have the same genes – each cell containing all the body's genes.

Cell division happens incredibly fast for some cell types. New red cells for your blood are produced at the rate of two million every second of your life. Other cells are much longer-lived, especially the nerve cells in your brain and your main nerves. This is because the intricate patterns of connections and links between the nerve cells would be disturbed if they died too often. And the pattern of links and connections allows you to think, remember and behave.

divided loyalties

There are two main kinds of cell division. The one shown here is mitosis. All of the double-set of genes is copied before each division, so that each offspring cell receives its own full double-set of genes. The other kind of cell division is called meiosis, and it makes the egg and sperm cells for reproduction, as described on page 116.

1
The strands of DNA which carry this white blood cell's genes have already been duplicated. Each coils tightly to form a chromosome (red and pink).

2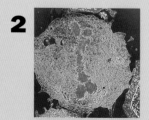
The two sets of chromsomes line up in the cell. A framework of microtubules, the mitotic spindle, prepares to pull them apart.

3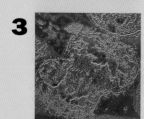
Each chromosome is pulled away from its partner, forming two separate sets of genetic information. The cell pinches around the middle.

4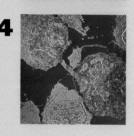
Division is almost complete as the two daughter cells redistribute their contents. The tiny connecting bridge breaks, and one cell has split into two.

Brain
Nerve cell in brain: 50 years.

Nose
Smell-sensing nose cell: 2 weeks.

Mouth
Flavour-sensing taste bud cell on tongue: 2 weeks.

Lymph node (gland)
White blood cell: 13 days.

Stomach
Lining cell: 2 days.

Skin
Skin cell: 4 weeks.

Blood
Red blood cell: 3 months.

Intestine
Intestinal lining cell: 12 hours.

Bone
Bone-making cell deep in bone: 20 years.

shapely cells

Not all cells are round balls. Some are long, thin rods, others are box-shaped, or flat like paving stones. A nerve cell has a more intricate shape. It has a blob near one end, the cell body. This is covered with dozens of small "tentacles" called dendrites. One part of the cell body is drawn out into a very long, thin, wire-like part – the axon. This cell shape enables the nerve cell to do its job of sending nerve signals from one part of the body to another.

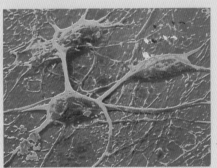

how old are you?

A machine like a personal stereo needs its batteries to be replaced often. The body also has often-replaced parts, especially certain cell types. To stay healthy, the body must replace cells as they die, with new ones made by cell division. On average, about 3,000 million cells in the body die every minute. They are replaced by 3,000 million new cells made by cell division, except for nerve cells in the brain, which die at the rate of 10,000 each day and are not replaced.

chapter

2

movement

FROM THE MOMENT you wake up in the morning and blink your eyes, to the time you yawn and go to sleep at night, your body is on the move. Your chest muscles make you breathe. Your head muscles make your facial expressions, and let you bite, chew and swallow. The muscles behind your eyeballs make them dart to and fro. Muscles of the larynx in the neck help you to speak, while other neck muscles support and move your head. Your arm and hand muscles let you grasp, hold and manipulate. Your leg and

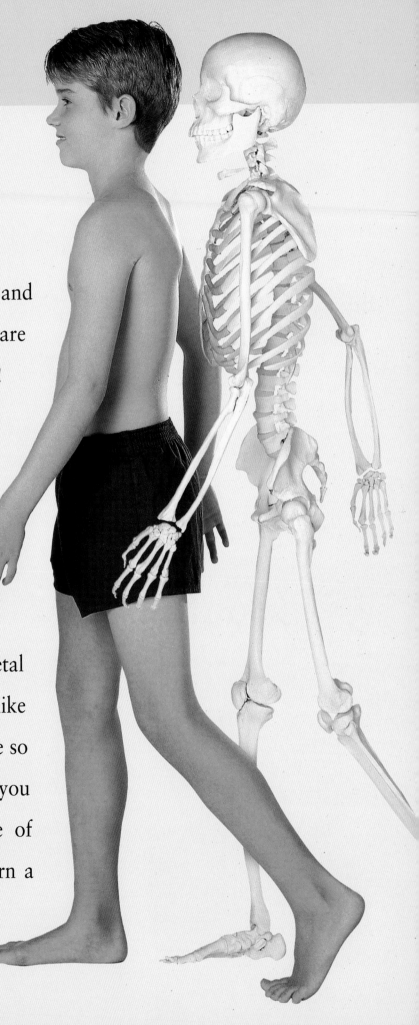

feet muscles make you walk and run, and perhaps kick. At no time during the day are you perfectly still – or you would be dead!

All the body's movements are powered by muscles. Most of them work by pulling on the body's system of supporting levers – the rigid but jointed moveable inner framework of bones that we call the skeleton. You have more than 600 skeletal muscles, and even the smallest action, like pointing, uses dozens of them. But you are so skilled at controlling your muscles that you hardly ever think about their multitude of movements. Until, that is, you try to learn a new activity.

the flexible coat

WHEN YOU LOOK AT PEOPLE, you probably notice their trainers, skin and perhaps their hair. What colour is it? Is the skin smooth or bumpy, or lined and wrinkled? These features are prominent and may seem important, but they can say little about the person inside the skin. Anyway, the skin surface that you see is entirely dead. The microscopic cells that cover its surface, like tiny tiles on a giant roof, died about two weeks ago. They became toughened and hardened so that they can withstand wear and tear. These cells are continuously being worn away as you move about, get dressed, rub inside your clothes, wash and dry with a towel, and do other daily activities. The cells shower from the body at an average rate of 50,000 every minute. They are continuously replaced by more dead, hardened cells moving up from below.

Your own leather bodysuit

Skin is the body's outer coating. It is like living leather. The skins of animals, from which leather is made, are similar to our own. One of skin's many jobs is to protect. It keeps out wind and rain, though it is more showerproof than fully waterproof. It keeps out dirt and germs, and it keeps in body fluids. Skin also keeps out harmful rays from the sun. However, if exposed to too much sun too rapidly, it may become sunburned. The cushion-like layer beneath the skin, called subcutaneous fat, helps to protect against knocks and bumps, and insulates against too much heat or cold. Skin plays an active role in helping to control body temperature, and it also provides our sense of touch (see also pages 96–97).

Hair shaft

Sebaceous gland

Hair root and nerve endings

Subcutaneous (under-the-skin) fat

Underlying muscle

wrinklies

A baby's skin is young and fresh, and has plenty of elastin. As it becomes older, it is affected by wind, sun and rain. The number of microscopic elastin fibres also decreases. This means that the skin becomes less flexible, making lines and creases appear. This process is speeded by exposure, especially to the sun.

Smooth and supple

Another amazing feature of skin is that it is flexible and supple, like the very best-quality wet-suit. This allows the body to make its constant movements. If skin were thicker, it might give better protection. But it would probably crack and split at the places where it was stretched and squeezed most as you move about. Skin's suppleness is helped by its natural waxes and oils, such as sebum. These are made in tiny glands just below the surface, and ooze onto the surface to make it more water-resistant and pliable. We put waxes, polishes and creams onto leather for the same reason.

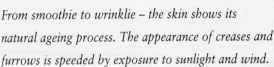

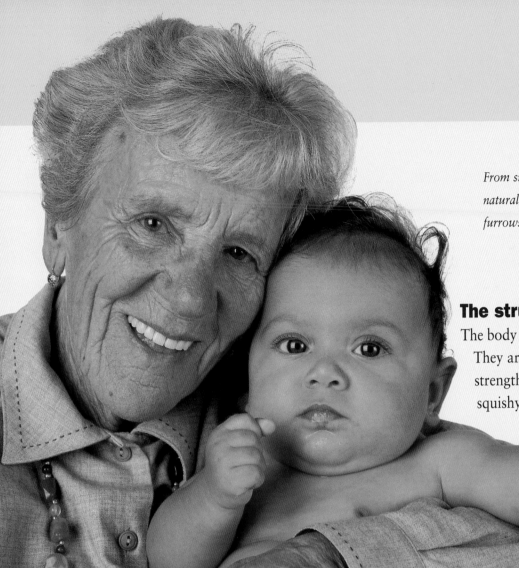

From smoothie to wrinklie – the skin shows its natural ageing process. The appearance of creases and furrows is speeded by exposure to sunlight and wind.

The structure of skin

The body contains hundreds of different proteins. They are its main structural molecules and give strength, shape and support to the softer, squishy bits. Skin's strength comes mainly from three proteins: keratin, collagen and elastin. They are in the form of microscopic string-like fibres. Keratin fills most of the cells that make up skin's outer layer, the epidermis. It is keratin that makes the cells hard and tough, to resist wear and rubbing.

Under the epidermis is the dermis. This contains fibres of collagen and elastin, and lots more besides. Collagen provides the strength, so that skin cannot stretch too much and snap. The elastin fibres make the skin elastic and rubbery. This means it can stretch and then spring back into shape.

flexible friend

The surface of the skin is coated with dead, flattened cells that are hardened with keratin. The cells eventually curl and flake and fall off. Keratin also forms the bulk of hairs, which grow up from pits in the skin called follicles. Here and there on the skin's surface are mysterious-looking holes. These are sweat pores. Watery sweat oozes through the pores from sweat glands below, to help cool the body. This microscope photograph shows male skin and facial hair sliced by a razor, surrounded by flaking, flattened cells of the outermost epidermal layer.

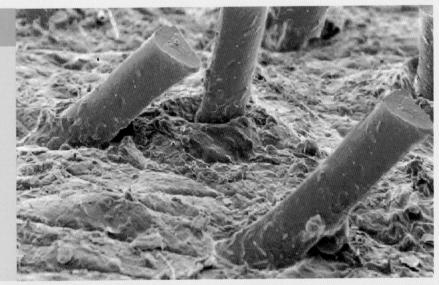

the skeleton

WHEN PEOPLE EAT TOO LITTLE for too long they become "skeletally thin". The fat and muscles shrink away, and the bones stand out under the skin. Even in such terrible circumstances, the body retains its main shape because of the nature of its bones.

The skeleton is the body's supporting framework. Its bones are very strong yet light, and perfectly shaped for their jobs. These include giving strength and rigidity to the floppier parts around them; being anchoring points for the ends of muscles; and acting as stiff levers for the muscles to pull on, and move the body about. The skeleton's main supporting structure is the backbone, or vertebral column, which runs through the centre of the body. The backbone consists of 7 neck vertebrae, 12 chest vertebrae, 5 middle-back vertebrae, 5 fused lower-back vertebrae and 3–5 fused "tail" vertebrae.

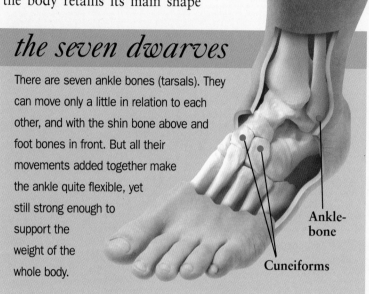

the seven dwarves

There are seven ankle bones (tarsals). They can move only a little in relation to each other, and with the shin bone above and foot bones in front. But all their movements added together make the ankle quite flexible, yet still strong enough to support the weight of the whole body.

Ankle-bone

Cuneiforms

Flexible joints that take the strain

Bones would not allow any movement if they were fixed firmly together, so they are linked at flexible joints (see page 34). Some bones are also protective. They form cases, cages and bowls. The rounded bones of the upper part of the skull, known as the cranium, form a hollow casket for the delicate brain. The curved bones of the eye sockets house the eyes. The ribs make a cage around the lungs and heart. And the hipbone, or pelvis, is a bowl that cradles the soft organs such as the bladder, the intestines and (in females) the womb.

Each bone has a scientific name. Indeed, every bump and hollow and projection on a bone has an anatomical name. These names are used by doctors, surgeons and other medical specialists, especially orthopaedic surgeons who specialize in problems affecting the bones and joints. Most bones also have everyday names. For example, the tibia is the shinbone, and the tarsals are the anklebones. The clavicle is the collarbone and has several lumps for muscle attachment. Some general parts of the body take their name from nearby bones. The side of the forehead is called the temple, from the temporal bone which forms the part of the skull beneath it. And bones also give their names to nearby nerves, blood vessels and other parts. The main blood vessel taking blood down to the leg is the femoral artery, named from the femur or thighbone close by.

handy movement

The forearm bones (radius and ulna) turn and twist slightly against each other. This lets you twist your wrist and hand, while keeping your elbow almost still.

Ulna

Radius

Radius

Ulna

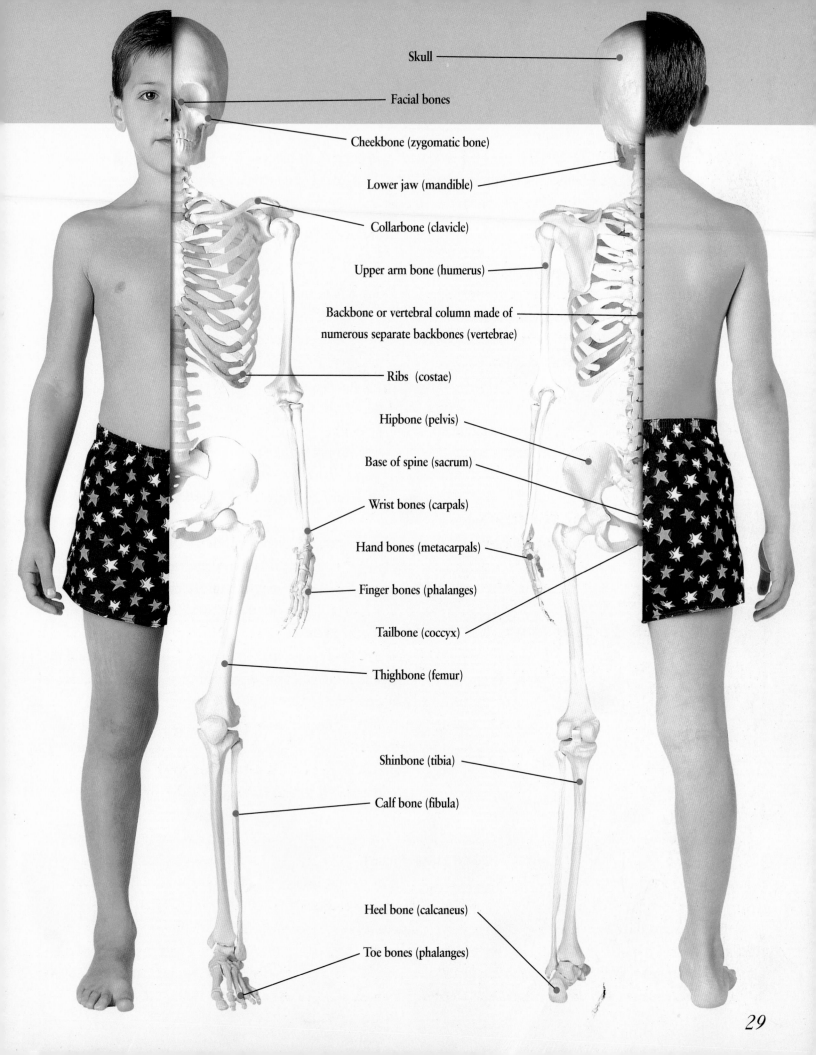

Skull

Facial bones

Cheekbone (zygomatic bone)

Lower jaw (mandible)

Collarbone (clavicle)

Upper arm bone (humerus)

Backbone or vertebral column made of
numerous separate backbones (vertebrae)

Ribs (costae)

Hipbone (pelvis)

Base of spine (sacrum)

Wrist bones (carpals)

Hand bones (metacarpals)

Finger bones (phalanges)

Tailbone (coccyx)

Thighbone (femur)

Shinbone (tibia)

Calf bone (fibula)

Heel bone (calcaneus)

Toe bones (phalanges)

inside bones

A BONE IS NOT COMPLETELY STIFF and rigid, as though made of steel. Nor is it totally solid, like a block of concrete. And neither is it brittle and flaky, like the long-dead bones you may see in museums. Living bones are slightly soft and flexible, partly hollow, smooth and resilient, and as busy with chemical life processes as any other part of the body.

A typical bone is actually made of two types of bony tissue. On the outside is a type of "skin" called the periosteum. Below this is a thin layer of thick, dense, "solid" bone. It is known as hard or compact bony tissue. Inside this, and forming the bulk of the middle of the bone, is a different bony tissue, more like a sponge or honeycomb. It has gaps and spaces, and it is called spongy, or alveolar, bony tissue. It is much lighter than the outer compact bone, and the spaces are filled with blood vessels, jelly-like bone marrow for making new blood cells (see page 66), and fat. This double-bony design gives great strength, yet saves weight. A skeleton made of steel would weigh five times more.

If you look at these bony tissues under a microscope, you see that they are made of bunches of minute rods jammed together. Each rod is known as a haversian system (after an English physician, Clopton Havers). It's like a tiny tree trunk, made of lots of even thinner layers, which show as rings when cut through. In the rod's central hole is an incredibly small set of blood vessels and nerves. These feed the innermost parts of the bone with nutrients, and detect pain and other problems.

Tough, but one-quarter water

If you carried out a chemical study on bone, then you might be surprised to find that this tough, hard substance is about one-quarter water! Around one-third consists of fibres of the protein collagen, which are also found in the skin, as described on page 26. Another one-third of bone is crystals made from calcium, phosphorus and other minerals. The collagen gives bone its slight elastic resilience, while the mineral crystals make it tough and rigid.

Bones are not isolated in the body, separate from all the other parts. Blood vessels and nerves pass through holes in their surface to reach the parts deep inside. Healthy bones contain lots of minerals. In times of shortage, some of these minerals can be dissolved out of the bone and carried away by the blood stream to wherever they are

(see page 66)

cold shoulder

The shoulder blade (scapula) is a broad, triangular plate of bone. It has a cup-shaped hollow for the end of the upper arm bone. It is joined by muscles to the ribs, collar bone and upper backbones, so that it can move from side to side and up and down. The movements of the shoulder blade help to make the shoulder a very flexible joint.

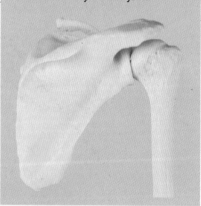

knee shield

The kneecap (patella) is a small sesamoid bone – one that is not attached directly to any other bone. It protects the front of the knee joint, and slides up and down as you bend and straighten your leg. Feel it!

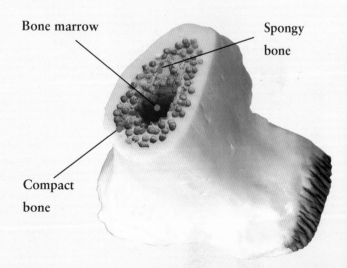

Bone marrow

Spongy bone

Compact bone

A slice through a long bone's shaft shows the internal structure.

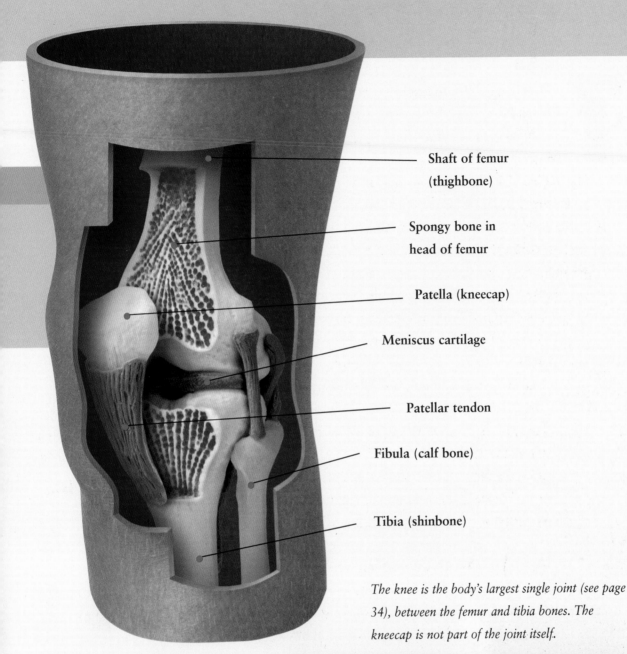

Shaft of femur
(thighbone)

Spongy bone in
head of femur

Patella (kneecap)

Meniscus cartilage

Patellar tendon

Fibula (calf bone)

Tibia (shinbone)

The knee is the body's largest single joint (see page 34), between the femur and tibia bones. The kneecap is not part of the joint itself.

(see page 34)

needed more urgently. This is one reason why certain diseases make bones become weakened and brittle. The same may happen with age, so the bones of an older person are less likely to bend under stress and more likely to snap. On the plus side, bones respond well to extra use and reasonable stresses. As you take exercise, your bones become stronger and more healthy, and better able to cope with the pressures and strains of movement.

x-ray vision

Bones show up as shadowy white shapes on a standard medical X-ray. Breaks, malformations and other oddities show up clearly too, as on this X-ray of a hand. The wrist is made up of eight small bones called carpals; the bones of the palm are called metacarpals.

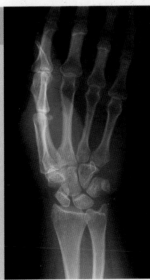

did you know?

► THE SKELETON MAKES UP ABOUT 1/7TH OF THE BODY'S TOTAL WEIGHT.

► THERE ARE 206 BONES IN THE AVERAGE BODY. BUT A FEW PEOPLE HAVE MORE, SUCH AS AN EXTRA PAIR OF RIBS, MAKING 13 PAIRS INSTEAD OF 12 AND THEREFORE 208 BONES IN ALL.

► THERE IS NO SCIENTIFIC BASIS FOR THE MYTH THAT MEN AND WOMEN HAVE A DIFFERENT NUMBER OF RIBS. THE MYTH MAY COME FROM THE BIBLE STORY ABOUT GOD CREATING WOMAN BY FASHIONING EVE FROM ADAM'S REMOVED RIB.

► THE LARGEST BONES ARE THE TWO FEMURS, OR THIGHBONES.

► THE SMALLEST BONES ARE THE STIRRUPS, TINY BONES ONLY 5–7 MILLIMETRES LONG, DEEP IN EACH EAR.

the skull and jaws

TAP YOUR KNUCKLES LIGHTLY on your head. Do you hear a hollow sound? Hopefully not, for the top half of your head is full of your brain. This vital organ is protected inside a curved casket – the bony braincase which forms the upper part of your skull. The skull is the name for the bony bits of the head and face. These bits are just under the skin, scalp and facial muscles. The skull is not one bone but more than 20. These began as separate curved shapes while you were in the womb, well before you were born, when your whole body could curl up and fit into a hen's egg. Gradually the bones grew by a process called osteogenesis (*osteo-* means to do with bones) and then began to join together. After birth, during childhood, the joints became firmly fixed along wiggly lines called sutures. So the resulting skull works like a single, strong piece of bone.

Occipital bone

Taking a look at the brainbox

The skull has an extremely intricate structure and design. The domed upper part, the braincase, is known as the cranium. It has eight large, curved sections that form the forehead, the temples, the crown of the head, and the bulging part at the rear. There are also several bones in its base, forming the roof of the mouth and the top of the neck. These bones have small holes in them to allow nerves and blood vessels to pass to the skin of the forehead and scalp.

Below and in front of the braincase are the 14 bones of your face. All have scientific names, and some have everyday names too. The zygomatic bone below the eye is known as the cheekbone. It is there not simply to make a face look beautiful, but to anchor the muscles which move the mouth, lips and jaws. On each side, parts of six bones form a bowl-shaped depression called the eye socket or orbit. This houses the eye, so that only the front third of the eyeball is exposed.

skull and crossbones

The skin over the skull is thin and soft, and well supplied with blood vessels. So it bleeds a lot if you get a cut there. Underneath the skin are the muscles of the face and scalp, which allow us to blink, bite, chew and make facial expressions. Then come the bones of the skull, which house and protect the delicate brain, eyes, nose and inner ears. In four sets of skull bones – the ethmoid, maxillary, sphenoid and frontal – there are air-filled chambers called sinuses. These are connected by holes and tubes to the main airways in the nose. One of the purposes of these air chambers is to help to make your voice sound louder.

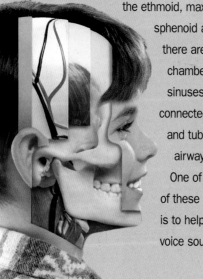

Nosing around

The skull has a hole for the nose. In life, the projecting part of the nose is made of flesh and the elastic substance called cartilage, or gristle. There are no true bones in the nose. After death, the cartilage rots away to leave a hole. Cartilage also forms the framework of the outer ear flap, which is why, after death, skulls are earless as well as noseless.

The largest single bone in the head is the lower jaw, or mandible. It is not strictly part of the skull, but a separate item. From the mandible and the upper jaw, which is made from two bones known as maxillae, grow your teeth. These are even harder than bone.

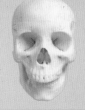

Parietal bone

A side view shows the main skull bones. The smaller bones in the face can only be seen from the front or below.

Frontal bone

Sphenoid bone

Orbital cavity

Lacrimal bone

Zygomatic bone (cheekbone)

Maxilla (upper jaw)

Hole in temporal bone for ear canal

Anterior fontanelle

Temporal bone

Mandible (lower jaw)

Jaw joint

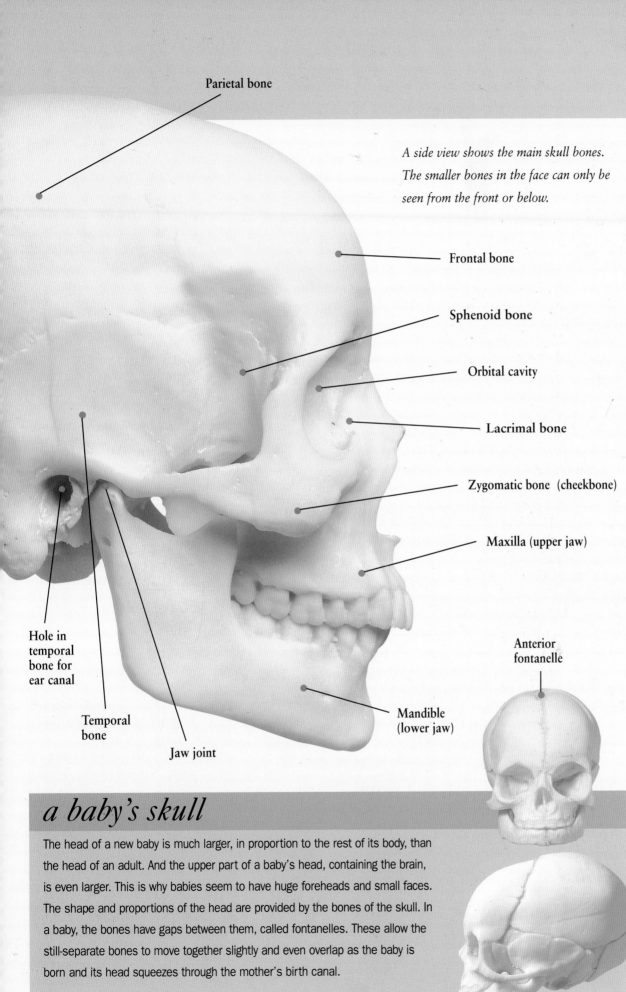

a baby's skull

The head of a new baby is much larger, in proportion to the rest of its body, than the head of an adult. And the upper part of a baby's head, containing the brain, is even larger. This is why babies seem to have huge foreheads and small faces. The shape and proportions of the head are provided by the bones of the skull. In a baby, the bones have gaps between them, called fontanelles. These allow the still-separate bones to move together slightly and even overlap as the baby is born and its head squeezes through the mother's birth canal.

joints and movement

hinge joint

The knee joint lets the lower leg swing to and fro, as shown by this tennis player. The hinge design gives limited movement but great strength. The knee is unusual because it has straps of ligaments called cruciate (cross-shaped) ligaments inside the joint, as well as ligaments around the outside (see page 31). Also it has two crescent-shaped pieces of cartilage, called menisci, that "float" between the bone ends. They give added stability and help to lock the knee straight so that you can stand up for long periods. People who sprint, twist and turn fast on their legs sometimes tear the cruciate ligaments or damage the menisci cartilages. If the cartilage in any joint becomes stiff and flaky and rough, this causes the painful condition of arthritis (*arthro* means to do with joints).

F THE BONES OF YOUR SKELETON were joined together solidly and rigidly, you would be completely stiff and unable to move. If the bones were not joined at all, your body would be stretchy and floppy as the bones came apart. Luckily, none of this happens. Your bones are linked by flexible joints that allow the bones to move in relation to each other, but also stop the bones separating.

Joints come in many sizes and designs. We give these different names, which come from the mechanical joints that we make for our machines and buildings. The ball-and-socket design is found in the shoulder and the hip. It is similar to the ball-and-socket joints in a car's suspension or in the base of a computer joystick. The ball-shaped head of a long bone, in the upper arm or thigh, fits into a cup-shaped socket in a large, flat bone – the shoulder blade or hipbone. This joint allows lots of movement because the long bone can swivel in any direction, to and fro and from side to side, and even twist lengthways.

Stability versus mobility

The hinge joint design is seen mainly in the elbow, knee and jaw. It works like the hinge on a door, and the joint can move only to and fro, not from side to side. The hinge joint makes up for this lack of flexibility by being very strong. This is true of most joints. The more flexible and mobile they are, the less strong and stable they are likely to be. A few joints allow no movement at all. They include the sutures between the bones of the skull. Other joints allow only a small amount of movement between their bones, but over lots of joints this adds up to great flexibility. The bones in the wrist, ankle and spinal column (backbone) work like this.

Although there is great variety in the size and shape of body joints, most of them have the same basic structure. This is called the synovial joint. The ends of the bones are held together by tough straps called ligaments. These bridge the gap between the bones and are anchored onto them at each end. Where bone ends move against each other, they are covered with cartilage, or gristle. This is shiny, smooth and slightly rubbery. It lets the bone ends slide past each other, with hardly any wear and tear. And it can absorb pressure and shocks when bones are forced together, as when you jump. If bare bones were pressed together, they would soon wear away. Under the ligaments is a flexible bag, the joint capsule. The inner lining of this bag is the synovial membrane. It continuously makes a slippery fluid called synovial fluid. This bathes the cartilage and acts as "oil" in the joint, to keep it working smoothly for many years.

ball and socket

Your shoulder joint lets you move your arm in almost any direction, as shown by this boy. The shoulder is a ball-and-socket design. But it has a very shallow socket on the shoulder blade, which allows the upper-arm bone to swivel and twist in almost any direction. The hip is similar, but has a deeper socket in the hip bone. So it is less flexible, yet stronger, for carrying the weight of the upper body.

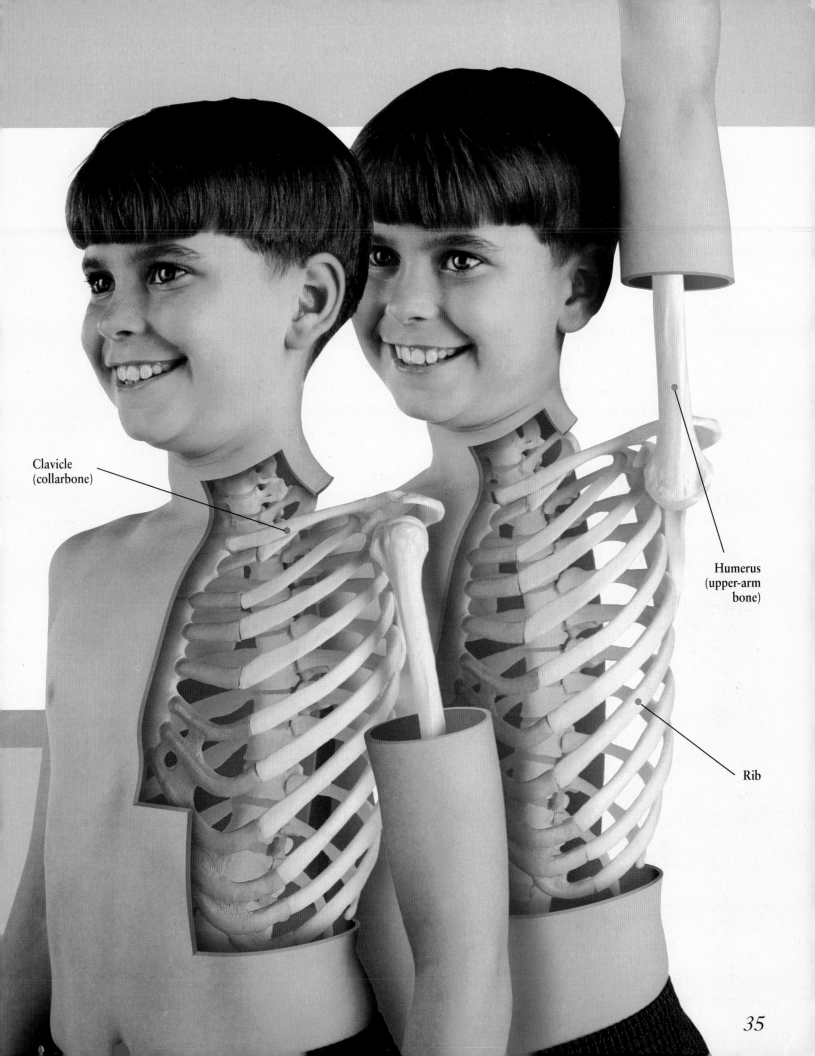

Clavicle
(collarbone)

Humerus
(upper-arm
bone)

Rib

muscles

AS YOU LIE IN BED AT NIGHT, trying to sleep, you may think that you are totally relaxed. But some muscles never sleep. They are busy making your heart beat and your lungs breathe, and pushing food through your digestive system. These types of muscle are described on page 41. Here, we are interested in the muscles that do become relaxed and floppy as you sleep.

They are called skeletal muscles because they are joined to the bones of the skeleton. When they work, they move the body. They are also called voluntary muscles because they are under the brain's conscious or voluntary control. This means that you can make them work when you want to. You cannot do this with the muscles in your heart or intestines.

You have more than 640 separate skeletal muscles, which make up about two-fifths of your whole body weight. Like bones, each one has a scientific name. But unlike bones, few muscles have everyday names. The biceps is one muscle, which bulges in the upper arm. To be more correct, its full name is biceps brachii (arm biceps), since there is another biceps in the thigh, the biceps femoris.

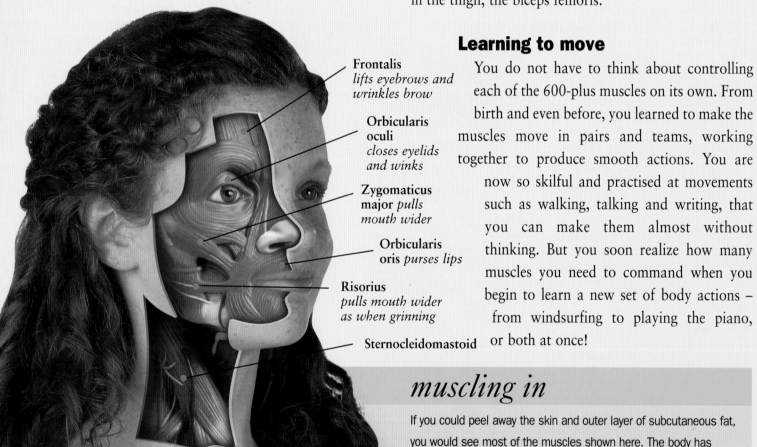

Frontalis
lifts eyebrows and wrinkles brow

Orbicularis oculi
closes eyelids and winks

Zygomaticus major *pulls mouth wider*

Orbicularis oris *purses lips*

Risorius
pulls mouth wider as when grinning

Sternocleidomastoid

Learning to move

You do not have to think about controlling each of the 600-plus muscles on its own. From birth and even before, you learned to make the muscles move in pairs and teams, working together to produce smooth actions. You are now so skilful and practised at movements such as walking, talking and writing, that you can make them almost without thinking. But you soon realize how many muscles you need to command when you begin to learn a new set of body actions – from windsurfing to playing the piano, or both at once!

muscling in

If you could peel away the skin and outer layer of subcutaneous fat, you would see most of the muscles shown here. The body has many other muscles, too, for this is only the outer layer. There are middle and deep layers beneath, criss-crossing each other and attaching to the bones at many different angles. There are other skeletal muscles as well, which are too small to show here.

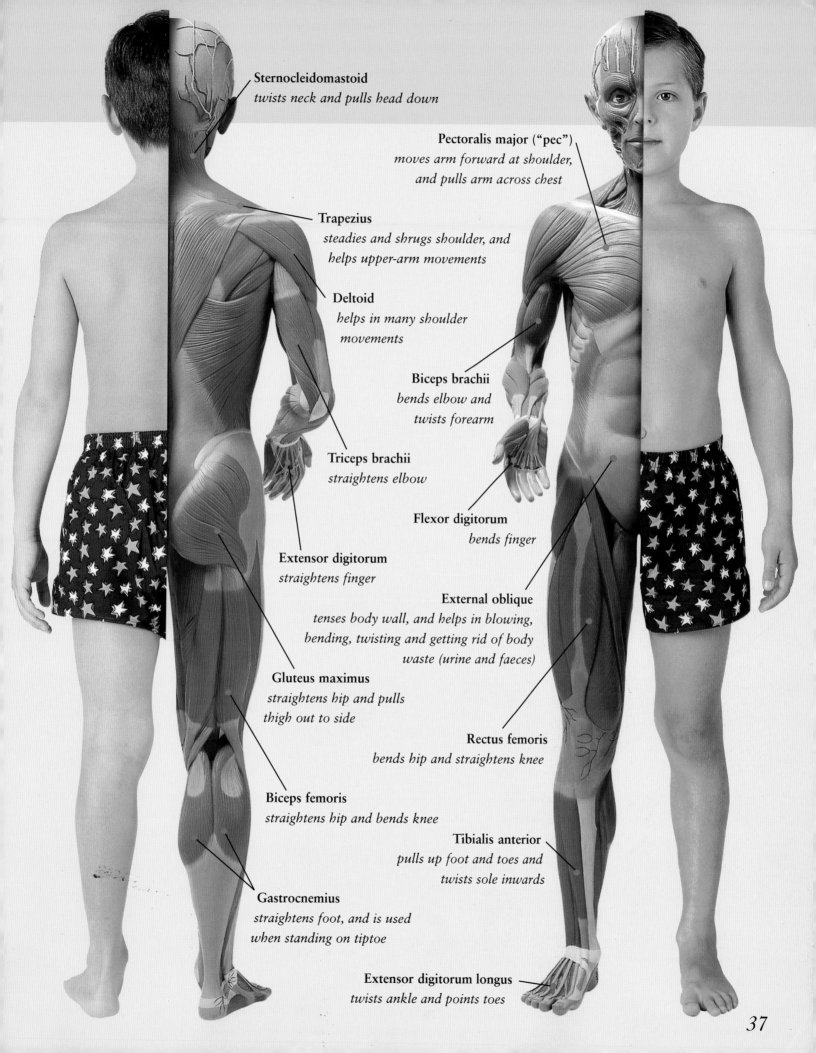

Sternocleidomastoid
twists neck and pulls head down

Pectoralis major ("pec")
*moves arm forward at shoulder,
and pulls arm across chest*

Trapezius
*steadies and shrugs shoulder, and
helps upper-arm movements*

Deltoid
*helps in many shoulder
movements*

Biceps brachii
*bends elbow and
twists forearm*

Triceps brachii
straightens elbow

Flexor digitorum
bends finger

Extensor digitorum
straightens finger

External oblique
*tenses body wall, and helps in blowing,
bending, twisting and getting rid of body
waste (urine and faeces)*

Gluteus maximus
*straightens hip and pulls
thigh out to side*

Rectus femoris
bends hip and straightens knee

Biceps femoris
straightens hip and bends knee

Tibialis anterior
*pulls up foot and toes and
twists sole inwards*

Gastrocnemius
*straightens foot, and is used
when standing on tiptoe*

Extensor digitorum longus
twists ankle and points toes

more about muscles

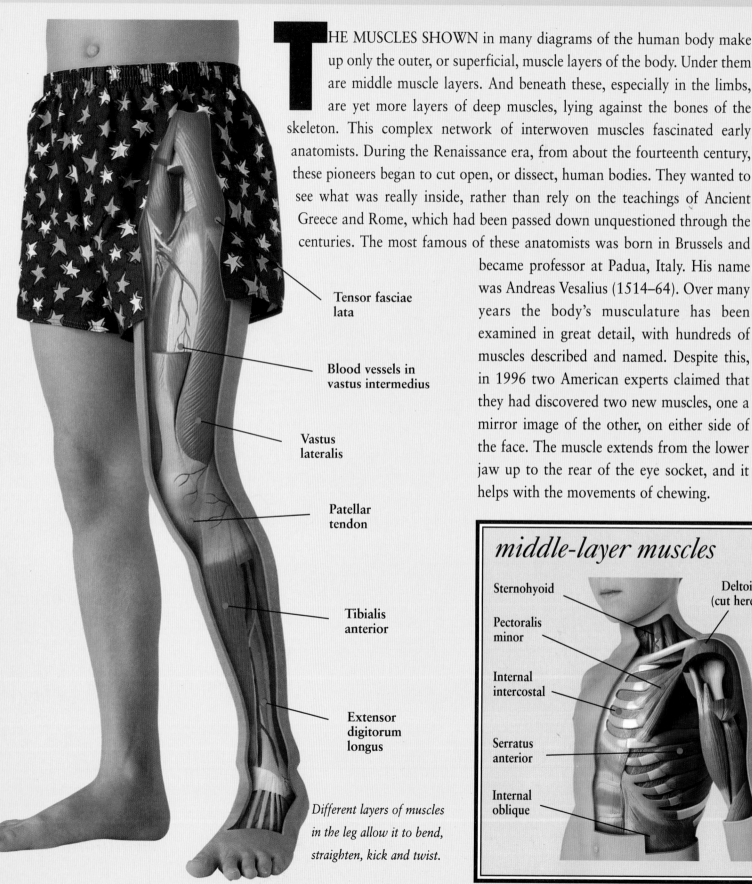

THE MUSCLES SHOWN in many diagrams of the human body make up only the outer, or superficial, muscle layers of the body. Under them are middle muscle layers. And beneath these, especially in the limbs, are yet more layers of deep muscles, lying against the bones of the skeleton. This complex network of interwoven muscles fascinated early anatomists. During the Renaissance era, from about the fourteenth century, these pioneers began to cut open, or dissect, human bodies. They wanted to see what was really inside, rather than rely on the teachings of Ancient Greece and Rome, which had been passed down unquestioned through the centuries. The most famous of these anatomists was born in Brussels and became professor at Padua, Italy. His name was Andreas Vesalius (1514–64). Over many years the body's musculature has been examined in great detail, with hundreds of muscles described and named. Despite this, in 1996 two American experts claimed that they had discovered two new muscles, one a mirror image of the other, on either side of the face. The muscle extends from the lower jaw up to the rear of the eye socket, and it helps with the movements of chewing.

Tensor fasciae lata

Blood vessels in vastus intermedius

Vastus lateralis

Patellar tendon

Tibialis anterior

Extensor digitorum longus

Different layers of muscles in the leg allow it to bend, straighten, kick and twist.

middle-layer muscles

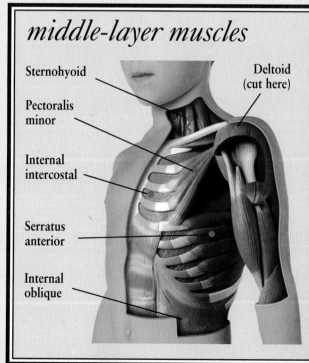

Sternohyoid

Pectoralis minor

Internal intercostal

Serratus anterior

Internal oblique

Deltoid (cut here)

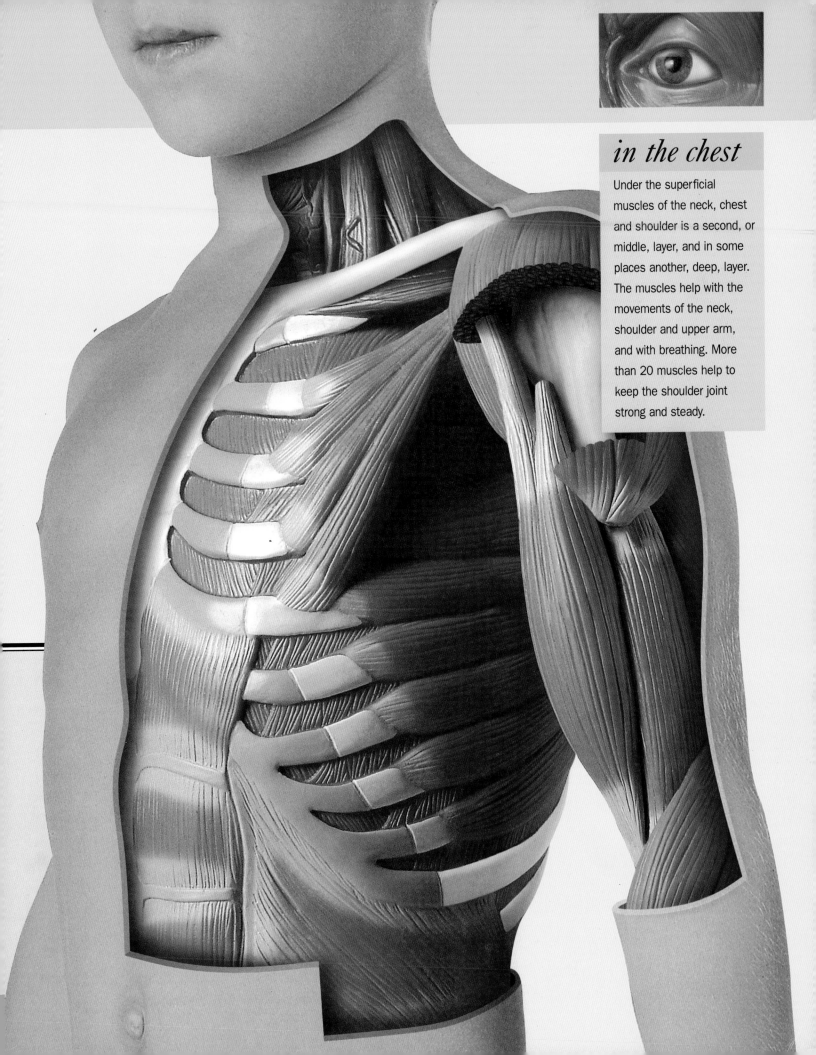

in the chest

Under the superficial muscles of the neck, chest and shoulder is a second, or middle, layer, and in some places another, deep, layer. The muscles help with the movements of the neck, shoulder and upper arm, and with breathing. More than 20 muscles help to keep the shoulder joint strong and steady.

inside muscles

As muscles tense and contract they bulge under the skin.

WHEN PEOPLE EAT BEEF STEAKS, they are consuming almost solid muscle – of a cow. Human muscles, and the muscles of most other mammals, are very similar in appearance and structure to those of the cow. When the animal is dead, the muscles are floppy lumps of red meat. But in life, muscles possess features that no other part of the body has. They can become tense and hard, and they can contract, or get shorter.

A typical muscle is long, bulging in the middle and tapered at the ends. Each end is attached to a bone by a tough, stringy extension of the muscle, called a tendon. The middle or belly of the muscle is built up from dozens of bundles of thin fibres known as myofibres (*myo-* means something to do with muscles). The thickest are as thin as hairs, while the slimmest are too thin to see. Myofibres vary in length according to the length of the whole muscle. In a very long muscle in the leg, they might be 10 cm (4 in) or even 30 cm (12 in) in length.

Giant cells give great power

Each myofibre is, in effect, a single cell – and therefore a giant compared to most other cells. It contains bundles of hundreds of even smaller string-like parts, known as myofibrils. In turn, these are made of bundles of even thinner, twisted, rope-like structures, the myofilaments. There are two types of myofilament. The thick ones are made of a body protein (structural substance) called myosin. The thin myofilaments are composed of another protein, actin. These myofilaments lie side by side, like pieces of rope put lengthways in a pile.

heave-ho!

As many people make small pulling movements, hand-over-hand on a rope, their efforts add up to give great strength and a long haul. Your muscle movements happen in the same way, adding up billions of molecular pulling actions between the myofilaments of actin and myosin.

smooth worker

Under the microscope, visceral muscle has a smooth or non-striped appearance. This is because the actin and myosin myofilaments are arranged at random, not in regular bundles. The dark spots are the dyed or stained nuclei (control centres) of each muscle cell.

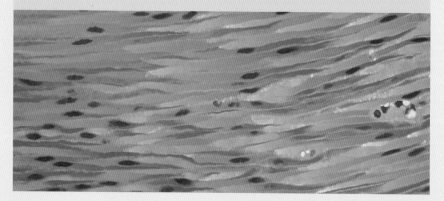

The main muscle molecules

Actin and myosin hold the key to muscle movement. A myosin myofilament has lots of stalks sticking out sideways from it. Each stalk has a ball-shaped head. This head grabs onto a nearby length of actin, and then the stalk bends and pulls the actin along. The head lets go and its stalk straightens. Then the head grabs the actin farther along, and the whole process repeats, to slide the actin a bit farther. It's like someone pulling hand-over-hand on a rope.

This process also happens with hundreds of other stalks on the myosin filament, as they haul

along their nearby actin myofilaments. It also occurs on hundreds of other myosin filaments in the myofibril, and with hundreds of other myofibrils in the myofibre, and with hundreds of other myofibres in the whole muscle. And so millions of the tiniest of movements, at the level of large molecules, add up to make the whole muscle contract.

Other types of muscle

In addition to skeletal or voluntary muscles, the body has two other main kinds of muscle. One is cardiac muscle, which makes up the walls of the heart. The other is visceral muscle. This forms layers in the walls of the viscera – the internal organs such as the stomach, intestines and bladder, as well as the walls of the main blood vessels.

Visceral muscle is also called involuntary muscle because its movements are involuntary, that is, you cannot control them. They work automatically. At the basic level, both cardiac and visceral muscles work in the same way as skeletal muscles, by bundles of actin and myosin. Cardiac muscle is specialized to contract regularly millions of times without fatigue or tiredness – otherwise the heart would stop! Visceral muscle is specialized to maintain pulling power or tension for long periods, and it is shaped into sheets, layers, bags and tubes to form the visceral organs.

muscle work-out

Under the microscope, skeletal muscle has a banded or striped appearance. This is because the actin and myosin myofilaments are arranged in regular bundles. Slide the fingers of one hand between those of the other hand, by about half their length. The area where the fingers overlap is like one of the dark bands in skeletal muscle, where the two sets of bundles overlap. This micro-photo is colour coded to show myosin myofilaments in orange and actin myofilaments in blue.

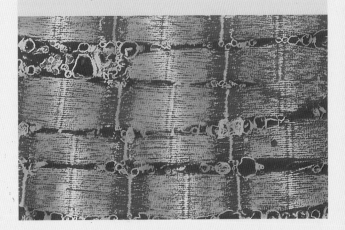

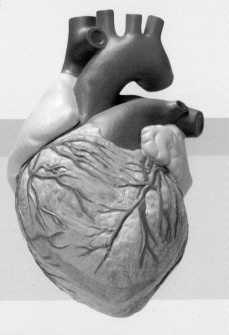

cardiac muscle

The heart's walls are made of cardiac muscle, also called myocardium. Its cells have a branching, bush-like pattern. Like any muscle, myocardium needs a plentiful blood supply. This is brought by the coronary arteries snaking over the outside of the heart. Myocardium is much thicker in the lower main pumping chambers, the ventricles.

making movements

Muscles move and balance the body in many ways!

MUSCLES ARE THE BODY'S MOVERS. Because of the way they work, with microscopic chemical hand-on-hand pulling like hauling a rope, muscles can only get shorter or contract. They are as useless at pushing, or getting forcefully longer, as you would be at pushing a rope. If muscles can only pull, how can your body push – and press, squeeze, crush and make all its other movements? The answer is that muscles work in pairs, and in larger groups or teams. For example, in your upper arm, the main muscle at the front is the biceps brachii. It tapers at its upper end into tendons anchored to the shoulder blade. At its lower end, its tapering tendons are fixed to the forearm bone called the radius, just below the elbow. When this muscle contracts, it pulls on the forearm bone and moves it. This bends your elbow. And this is how muscles work – by pulling bones.

Antagonistic partners

How do you straighten your elbow? The biceps muscle cannot help. It cannot push the forearm bone back again. If you are standing up straight, gravity can help by dragging your forearm and hand downwards. But the main power comes from the triceps brachii. This is in a similar position to the biceps, but on the other side of the upper arm. So when it contracts, it pulls the lower arm the other way. As this happens, the short and bulging biceps relaxes, and is pulled long and thin again.

The biceps and triceps are called opposing or antagonistic partners. All over the body, muscles are arranged in pairs like this. Look on page 38 at the thigh muscles. The biceps femoris and the rectus femoris are like the arm's biceps and triceps, but they work the knee. The biceps behind bends the knee, and the rectus femoris at the front straightens it, as when kicking. In many cases, these antagonistic pairs are part of even more complicated muscle groups. Some pull diagonally or at sharp angles. By their combined actions, they can pull bones to and fro, and twist or pivot them, to make the body's vast range of movements.

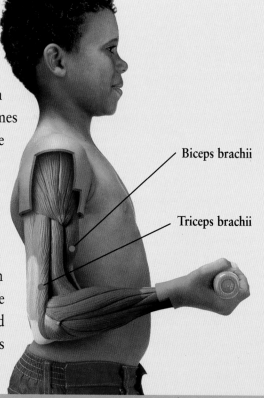

Biceps brachii

Triceps brachii

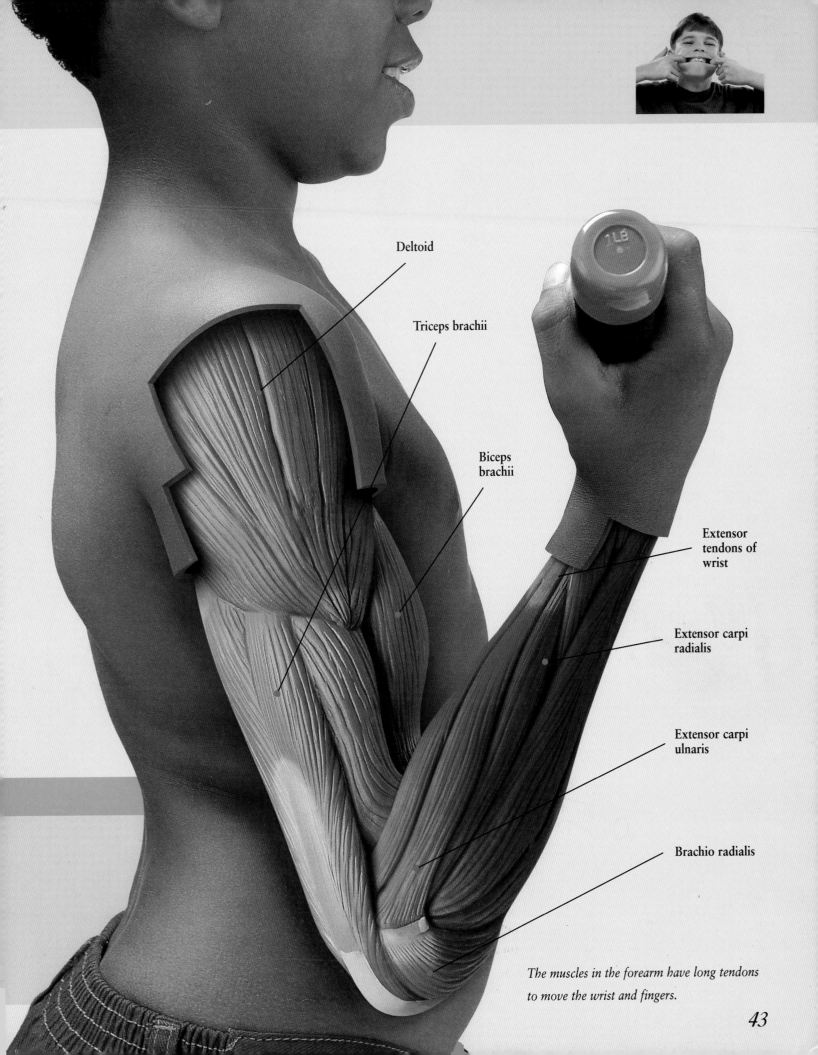

Deltoid

Triceps brachii

Biceps
brachii

Extensor
tendons of
wrist

Extensor carpi
radialis

Extensor carpi
ulnaris

Brachio radialis

*The muscles in the forearm have long tendons
to move the wrist and fingers.*

43

faces and fingers

MUSCLES POWER every body action, from lifting heavy weights and leaping high into the air, to the tiniest movement of the face or fingers. These small movements use only small muscles. In a little muscle, only a few hundred of the myofibres (see page 40) may be involved in the contraction.

Look in a mirror and make some faces at yourself. See how your eyebrow, eyelid or lip has to move only a few millimetres to change your facial expression entirely. We use these precise, delicate facial movements to convey our moods and feelings to others.

Other muscle anchors

There are about 50 main muscles in the face. Unusually, some of them are not connected to bones. Their ends are anchored on other muscles or on knobs or sheets of stringy, fibrous material (known as aponeuroses). There is a blob of this at each corner of the mouth, called the modiolus. It is the fixing point for the ends of eight muscles that go around the lips, up to the eye on that side, sideways to the cheek, and down to the lower cheek and chin.

Look in the mirror again. Smile, then widen your mouth in a grimace, and then frown. See how your face muscles pull the corner of your mouth up, then out, then down. Hold the corner of your mouth between thumb and forefinger, and you can feel the stringy lump of the modiolus just to the side, under the skin. As you do this, watch your finger and thumb, too.

the flexible tongue

The tongue is almost solid muscle, and is extremely flexible. It can change its shape and move in almost any direction. This allows you to form the sounds of clear speech, move food around when you eat and chew, and lick your lips afterwards. Six intrinsic lingual muscles form the tongue's main bulk. These are two superior longitudinals, which make the edges curl up into a U shape; two inferior longitudinals, which do the opposite, an upside-down U shape; a transverse muscle that changes the tongue's shape to long and thin; and a vertical muscle that makes it flat and wide. Embedded within the tongue are four sets of extrinsic muscles. The hyoglossus moves it down; the palatoglossus lifts it up; the styloglossus pulls it back; the genioglossus pokes it out – but be careful when you do this!

The faces on these pages are very exaggerated. Even tiny muscle movements that hardly change the face can show moods and emotions.

Finger movements

Your hands and fingers can make incredibly precise movements. Simply writing your name shows great control. Each finger has a long muscle that bends it. The muscle, called the flexor digitorum, is actually in the inside of the forearm. It is connected to the finger bones by a long tendon that runs through your wrist. Clench all your fingers hard into a fist and bend your wrist slightly, and you can see the muscles rippling under the skin of your forearm. Each of these muscles has an opposing partner called the extensor digitorum, on the outside of the forearm. Each is linked to the other sides of the finger bones by a long tendon running through the back of the wrist. Working in pairs, these muscles can straighten and flex the fingers, to the accuracy of one or two millimetres.

There are also sets of small muscles attached to the various finger bones in each finger, between each pair of knuckles. These add to the precision and dexterity of hand actions. When you were a baby, you gradually learned how to control all of these muscles so that you could grasp, grab, hold, squeeze, clench, pinch, flick, draw, write and make all the other movements which you now take for granted.

gripping stuff

The human hand has three main types of grip. One is the hook grip, which you use if you are hanging from a bar or pulling a door. Another is the power grip, used to hold a screwdriver or a tennis racquet in the palm. The third is the precision grip, which generally means putting the item between the tips of thumb and forefinger, as when threading a needle or picking up a pin. These grips depend largely on the position of the most mobile digit, the first one of the five – the thumb. It has a very flexible saddle-type joint at its base, and several muscles pulling at different angles on its three bones, so that you can move its tip right around in a wide circle. Only apes and monkeys also have a thumb with such extraordinary flexibility, but no other animal can match the range of movements of the human hand.

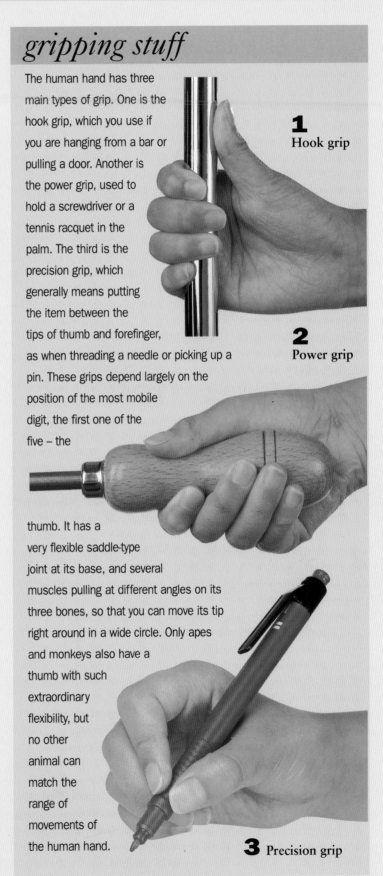

1 Hook grip

2 Power grip

3 Precision grip

chapter

3

food and energy

OUR MODERN world depends on two great resources: energy and raw materials. We use many different forms of energy, such as coal, gas, oil, nuclear power and hydro-power (running water). These are often converted into electricity, which can be sent along wires for use in homes, schools, factories, shops and other places. Our world also uses hundreds of raw materials for building and making things, including metals like iron, steel and aluminium, as well as stones, bricks, woods and plastics.

The body needs the same two great resources: energy and raw

materials. These come from one source – food. Our food contains the energy we need to live. Like petrol in a car, food energy is in the form of chemicals such as sugars, starches and other carbohydrates. Food also contains many different raw materials, such as proteins and minerals, that our bodies need to grow and to maintain and repair themselves.

A N ELEPHANT EATS almost nothing but grass – all day and for most of the night, too. In its stomach, the elephant digests the grass, which means that the grass is broken down or disassembled into tiny pieces called molecules. These molecules pass into the elephant's intestines, get absorbed into the bloodstream and are carried all around the elephant's body. In its cells and tissues, the molecules are reassembled in different combinations to maintain and repair parts such as muscles, blood, bones, nerves, skin, and even tusks and trunk. The overall effect is that grass becomes elephant.

The same happens in your body. Whatever you eat – the whole A–Z of food, from apples, burgers and carrots, to yams and zucchinis – is changed into your body.

You are what you eat

Food contains the raw materials, or nutrients, that you need to grow. When you have finished growing, the raw materials keep your body maintained, repair injuries, and replace bits lost through normal wear and tear. Your digestive system digests your food, breaking it down into molecules, which are taken into your bloodstream. All over your body, these molecules are built up again in different combinations, to form your body tissues, just like the elephant (except for the tusks and trunk). The overall effect is that food becomes you.

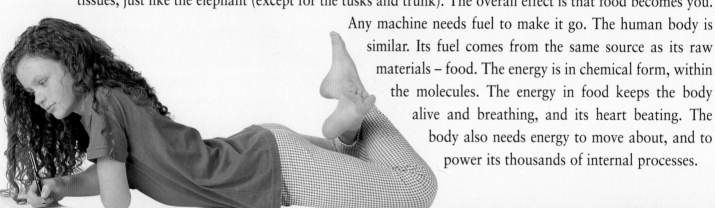

Any machine needs fuel to make it go. The human body is similar. Its fuel comes from the same source as its raw materials – food. The energy is in chemical form, within the molecules. The energy in food keeps the body alive and breathing, and its heart beating. The body also needs energy to move about, and to power its thousands of internal processes.

pick and mix

People around the world eat different traditional foods. In some places, rice forms the main part of each meal, in others cassava (manioc), potatoes, or bread. In some regions, fish and seafood are popular, while in others, poultry or red meat are more common. Some people eat no meat at all. The important factor is to eat lots of different foods. Fresh vegetables, fruits and salads are especially healthy.

food energy

ABOUT ENERGY

In science, energy is usually measured in joules. One joule is a very small unit, so the energy in food is measured in thousands of joules. 1,000 joules is written as 1 kJ (kilojoule). In the past the unit for measuring the energy in food was the Calorie (Cal or kc). 1 kJ (kilojoule) equals 0.24 Calories (Cals or kilocalories). However, today we mainly use kJ. Look at the 'nutrition information' box on various packaged foods to see how much energy they contain.

HOW MUCH ENERGY DO YOU USE?

Sitting or lying – 3–5 kJ per minute

Walking – 10–15 kJ per minute

Running – 30–40 kJ per minute

AVERAGE ENERGY USES PER DAY

Average 10-year-old child – 7,000 kJ

Inactive person (desk job) – 8,500 kJ

Fairly active person (teacher) – 11,000 kJ

Very active person (athlete) – 15,000 kJ

A balanced diet

Some foods are high in energy. Others are rich in raw materials. Some contain both energy and raw materials, and the body uses them according to its needs. To stay healthy, the human body needs a wide variety of foods from many sources, called a balanced diet. Too much of any single food is bad for you.

eating a balanced diet

The human body has evolved over thousands and millions of years so that it needs certain kinds of food. We cannot survive on grass alone, unlike an elephant. To stay healthy, we need a varied diet which provides all the essential substances and not too much fat, especially animal fats, which can be unhealthy.

CARBOHYDRATES Mainly for energy. Found in sugary and starchy foods such as potatoes, wheat, rice and other cereals, pasta, bread, some fruit and vegetables.

PROTEINS Mainly for growth, building new body tissues, maintenance and repair. Found in meat, poultry, fish, dairy products, beans and similar pulses, as well as grains and cereals.

FATS Mainly for energy and for building, maintaining and repairing some body tissues, like nerves. Found in dairy products, many red meats, some poultry and fish, and oily plant foods such as peanuts and avocados.

VITAMINS AND MINERALS Essential in small quantities for growth, maintenance and repair, and the smooth running of the body's chemical processes. They include iron for the blood and calcium for teeth and bones. Found in many foods, especially fresh fruits and vegetables.

FIBRE (roughage) Found in most wholegrains, fruit and vegetables. It cannot be digested, but provides bulk and greatly helps the digestive process.

WATER Essential for all life (see page 72).

AMOUNTS OF ENERGY IN COMMON FOODS

Portion of sprouts – 90 kJ	Chocolate bar – 1,000 kJ
Portion of carrots – 100 kJ	Portion of chips – 1,300 kJ
Small apple – 170 kJ	Portion of salami slices – 500 kJ
Portion of fresh peas – 200 kJ	Cucumber garnish – 20 kJ
Slice of bread – 200–250 kJ	Boiled egg – 300 kJ
Banana – 270 kJ	Teaspoon of honey – 60 kJ
Grilled low-fat burger – 350 kJ	Thumb-sized cheese chunk – 400 kJ
Grilled chicken leg – 600 kJ	Doughnut – 1,500 kJ

our daily bread

WHEN YOU FEEL "STARVING", you might eat food very quickly. But the time you take to eat has little effect on the time your digestive system takes to break down, absorb and process food. If you are really rushed, you might not even chew each mouthful properly, thinking that this will speed things along. But it does not. Your stomach has to spend extra minutes squashing the food, doing the job that your teeth did not do thoroughly. The stomach is one of the main parts of the digestive system. The system consists of a long tube, the digestive tract, with some parts wider than others. Each part does its own job in the whole process of digestion. As the food moves through the digestive tract, it meets the mouth, teeth and tongue, the throat, the oesophagus (or gullet), the stomach, the small intestine, the large intestine, and the anus, which is the final opening for wastes and leftovers to emerge back into the outside world.

A moving story

Food is pushed along the digestive tract by squeezing motions made by the muscles in the walls of the tract, rather as if you squeezed jelly along a hosepipe with your hands. This powerful rhythmic squeezing motion is called peristalsis. If you swallow food that is bad in some way, such as poisonous berries, peristalsis in the oesophagus and stomach can go into reverse, pushing the food back up and out again with great force. We know this as being sick, or vomiting. It may be unpleasant, but it's helpful – one of the body's many self-protecting mechanisms against damage and disease. As the old saying describes it: "Better out, than in."

The liver and pancreas are also included in the digestive system. They are not parts of the long digestive tube, or tract, but they are very involved in the process of digestion, as you can read over the following pages.

Good daily digestion

How long does it take to digest a meal? It depends on how much you eat, the types of food, and how long you chew it. In general, fatty foods take longer to digest than other foods. On average, the whole process takes 24–36 hours. So each main meal you eat spends about a day inside your digestive system. At the end are the leftovers – brown, squidgy faeces or bowel motions (stools). They are bits of food that cannot easily be digested, such as fibre, along with bits of rubbed-off lining from the stomach and intestines.

the digestive tract

- ➤ **Mouth** – the first stop for food while it is being chewed and softened.
- ➤ **Tongue** – moves food around the mouth for thorough chewing and pushes it to the back of the mouth for swallowing. The tongue also tastes – and may detect if food is bad to spit it out!
- ➤ **Teeth** – chop and chew food into smaller, softer lumps for swallowing.
- ➤ **Salivary glands** – make saliva (spit) that mixes with the food to make it moist and squishy, and starts digestion with its enzymes.
- ➤ **Lips** – seal together to stop food and drinks dribbling out of the mouth.
- ➤ **Throat (pharynx)** – receives swallowed food and pushes it into the top of the oesophagus.
- ➤ **Oesophagus** – pushes food by waves of peristalsis down into the stomach.
- ➤ **Stomach** – writhes and squirms to squash and mash food, and bathes it with chemicals (acids and enzymes) to break it down.
- ➤ **Small intestine** – adds more digestive chemicals and absorbs the digested nutrients into the body.
- ➤ **Large intestine** – takes in excess water and minerals from the leftover food, and forms the waste into faeces.
- ➤ **Rectum** – stores the faeces until a convenient moment.
- ➤ **Anus** – opens to let the faeces pass out of the digestive tract.

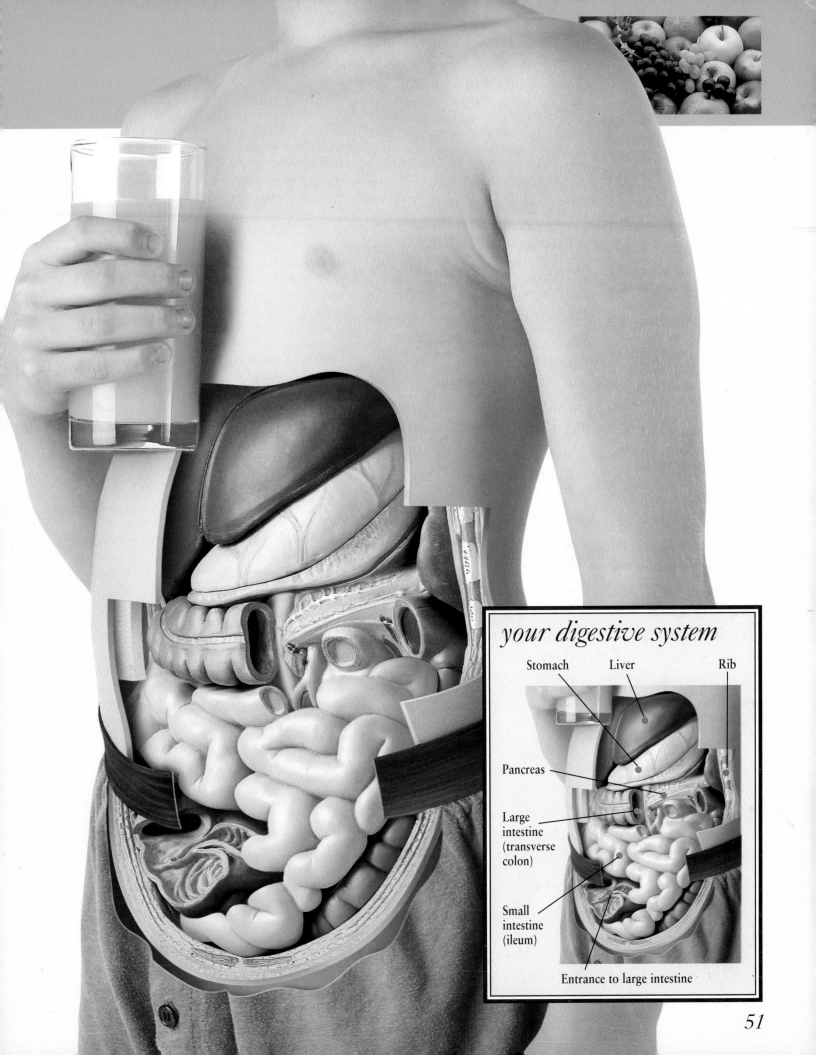

your digestive system

Stomach   Liver   Rib

Pancreas

Large
intestine
(transverse
colon)

Small
intestine
(ileum)

Entrance to large intestine

51

bite and chew

YOUR TEETH CHOP FOOD INTO BITE-SIZED PIECES, and mash and chew these into lumps of soft pulp, which can be swallowed more easily. How many teeth have you got? It depends partly on your age, and also on whether you brush them regularly and keep your teeth and gums clean. If you don't look after your teeth they may go bad and decay. They may even have to be taken out by the dentist. Teeth are not all the same. They have different sizes and shapes, and do different jobs. The front ones, incisors, are slim, wide-ended and sharp, like small chisels or spades. They cut and slice. The ones behind are the canines. They are more pointed, like tiny daggers, and good for tearing and ripping foods. At the back are the premolars and molars, which are wide and fairly flat. They crush and squash the food when chewing.

Two sets of teeth for everyone

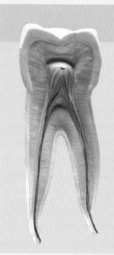

Regular visits to the dentist are important for healthy teeth.

The average person has two sets of teeth, one after the other. The first is the baby, milk or deciduous set. Even before birth, teeth appear as tiny buds below the gums. They begin to erupt, or show above the gum, from the age of a few months. By the age of about three, all 20 first teeth have usually appeared. In each half (left and right) of each jaw (upper and lower) there are two incisors, one canine and two molars.

From about six years of age, the first teeth fall out. These are replaced by the adult, second or permanent set. First are usually the front incisors and the first molars, at around seven to eight years. Last are the rearmost molars, or wisdom teeth. These appear at 18–20 years in some

inside a tooth

Each tooth has two main parts. The root anchors it firmly in the gum, to withstand the tremendous pressures that are exerted when you bite and chew hard foods like nuts. The crown is the visible part above the gum. It is covered with whitish enamel, which is the hardest substance in the entire body. Under the enamel is a layer of dentine, which is not quite so hard, and absorbs shocks and knocks. In the centre of the tooth are blood vessels, providing nourishment to the tooth's parts and layers, and nerves, to detect pressure and pain.

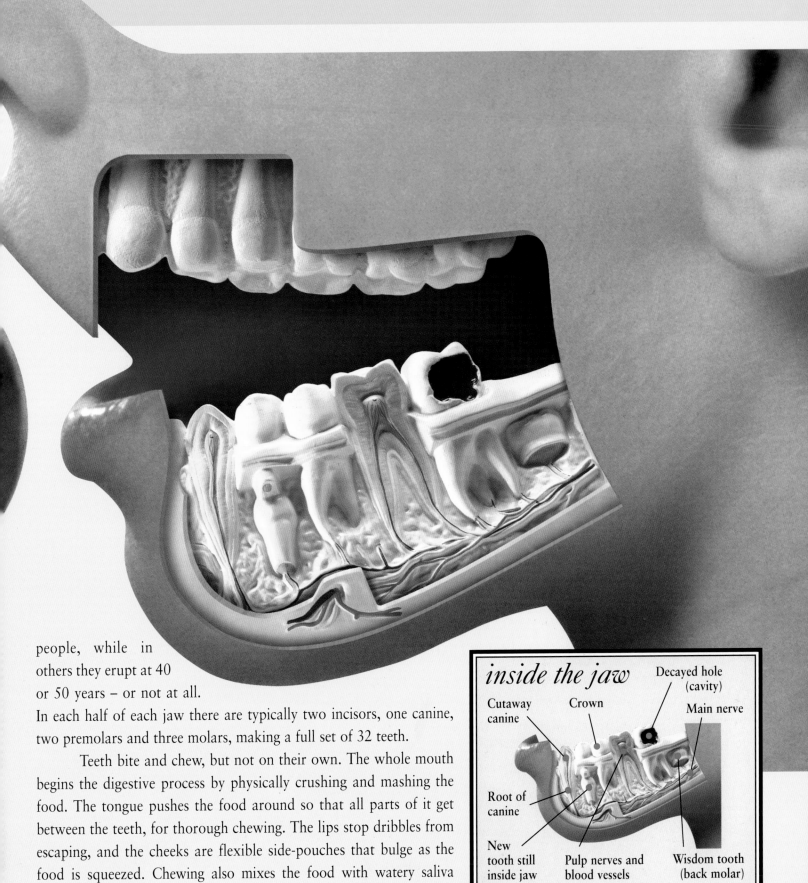

people, while in others they erupt at 40 or 50 years – or not at all.

In each half of each jaw there are typically two incisors, one canine, two premolars and three molars, making a full set of 32 teeth.

Teeth bite and chew, but not on their own. The whole mouth begins the digestive process by physically crushing and mashing the food. The tongue pushes the food around so that all parts of it get between the teeth, for thorough chewing. The lips stop dribbles from escaping, and the cheeks are flexible side-pouches that bulge as the food is squeezed. Chewing also mixes the food with watery saliva (spit), which makes it easier to swallow and starts the digestive process.

inside the jaw

Cutaway canine

Crown

Decayed hole (cavity)

Main nerve

Root of canine

New tooth still inside jaw

Pulp nerves and blood vessels

Wisdom tooth (back molar)

can you stomach it?

This is a microscopic view of a gastric pit in the stomach lining.

IF YOU DID NOT HAVE A STOMACH, you could not eat just two or three main meals each day. You would have to eat lots of tiny ones much more frequently. The stomach is like a stretchy storage bag for food. It expands to hold a whole meal. Then the layers of muscle in its walls contract to make it squeeze, first one way, then another. Meanwhile, tiny glands in the stomach lining release their digestive chemicals, including powerful food-corroding acids and strong nutrient-splitting enzymes. Under this combined physical and chemical attack, after a few hours the food has become a mushy part-digested soup.

Do you have the guts for this?

Around two to four hours after arriving in the stomach, the part-digested soup begins to leave. Small amounts trickle regularly from the stomach into the next section of the digestive tract – the small intestine. Here, more enzymes are added to the soup. They come from the intestine's own lining, and also along a tube from the nearby pancreas, which makes its own powerful digestive juices. The original substances in the food are broken down into smaller and smaller pieces. Proteins are broken down into small molecules called amino acids. Starches are broken down into small molecules known as sugars.

Finally the food is fully broken down and digested. The resulting molecules are small enough to pass through the lining of the small intestine. They seep into the blood flowing through the lining and get carried away around the body in the bloodstream. Many are carried to the liver, which is a major food-processing and storage centre. The liver changes

barium meal

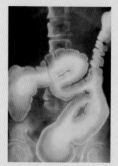

A normal X-ray photograph does not reveal the parts of the digestive system. However, a substance called barium shows up clearly on X-rays as a white area. If a person swallows a special fluid containing barium, this trickles into the digestive tract, fills it, and shows all its tubes, chambers, nooks and crannies. This "barium meal" can reveal problems such as ulcers, growths and blockages in the system. The X-ray above has had the white barium-filled parts of the intestine coloured in orange.

enlarging the small intestine

If you look very closely at the inner lining of the small intestine, it seems velvety or hairy. It is covered with thousands of tiny finger-shaped objects called villi. These form a much larger surface area, compared to a flat lining, for absorbing as much food as possible. Inside each villus are tiny blood vessels – capillaries – and also small tubes known as lacteals containing another body fluid, lymph. The nutrients pass into the villi and are carried away to the liver and around the body.

This cutaway view of the small intestine is about life-sized.

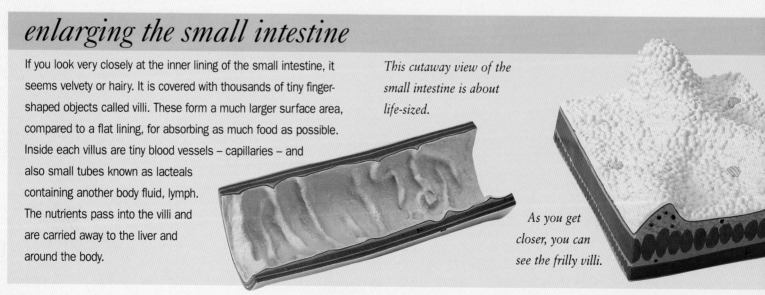

As you get closer, you can see the frilly villi.

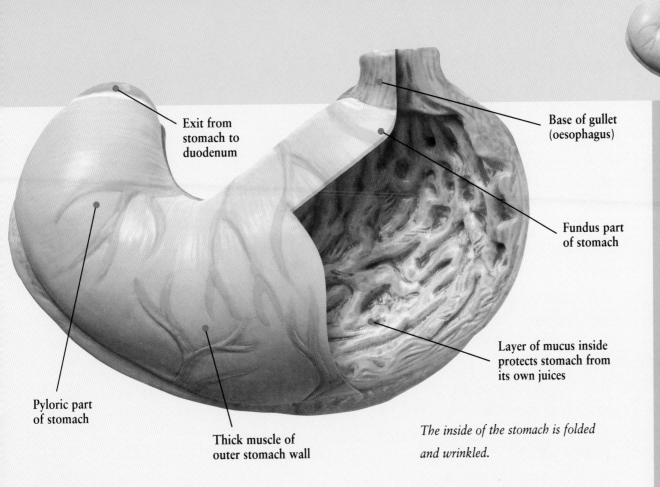

Exit from
stomach to
duodenum

Base of gullet
(oesophagus)

Fundus part
of stomach

Layer of mucus inside
protects stomach from
its own juices

Pyloric part
of stomach

Thick muscle of
outer stomach wall

*The inside of the stomach is folded
and wrinkled.*

*did you
know?*

THE LENGTHS OF THE
VARIOUS PARTS OF THE
DIGESTIVE TRACT VARY
WITH A PERSON'S SIZE
AND AGE. ON AVERAGE:

➤ THE OESOPHAGUS IS
AROUND 25 cm (10 in) LONG.

➤ THE STOMACH HOLDS
UP TO 2 LITRES (3.5 PINTS).

➤ THE SMALL INTESTINE
HAS THREE SECTIONS: THE
DUODENUM, JEJUNUM AND
ILEUM. IN TOTAL IT IS 5–6 m
(17–20 ft) LONG AND
3–4 cm (1–1½ in) WIDE.

➤ THE LARGE INTESTINE
(COLON) IS 1.5 m (5 ft)
LONG AND 5–8 cm
(2–3 in) WIDE.

➤ FOOD SPENDS AN
AVERAGE OF 24 HOURS IN
THE DIGESTIVE SYSTEM.
FATTY FOODS TAKE
LONGEST TO DIGEST.

➤ THE SURFACE AREA
OF THE GUT IS ROUGHLY
EQUIVALENT TO THE SIZE
OF A FOOTBALL PITCH!

certain nutrients into others, and stores sugars, vitamins and other substances. It also changes possibly harmful substances, such as some drugs, into safer, harmless versions.

Some parts of the original food cannot be digested. These leftovers and wastes trickle on from the small intestine into the large one. Here, water is absorbed from them, along with any useful minerals and body salts. Gradually the wastes and leftovers become semi-solid and form the faeces. These are stored in the next-to-last main part of the digestive tract – the rectum. Finally, at a convenient time and place, the faeces leave through the muscular opening at the end of the digestive tube, known as the anus.

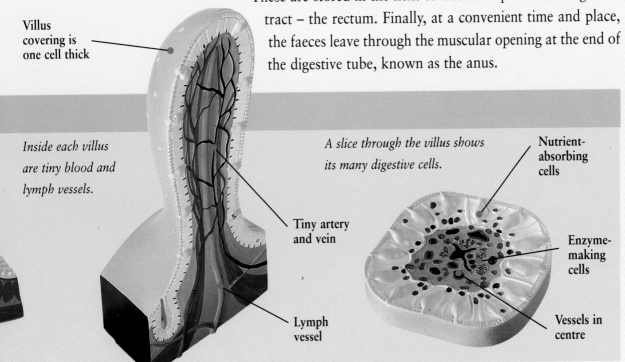

Villus
covering is
one cell thick

*Inside each villus
are tiny blood and
lymph vessels.*

Tiny artery
and vein

Lymph
vessel

*A slice through the villus shows
its many digestive cells.*

Nutrient-
absorbing
cells

Enzyme-
making
cells

Vessels in
centre

55

the vital breath

OXYGEN IS AN INVISIBLE GAS which makes up one-fifth of the air. It is a vital part of the chemical pathway that goes on inside the cells of living things, releasing energy from the nutrients in food. This chemical pathway is known as cellular respiration. It usually begins with molecules of the sugar called glucose, which come from digested carbohydrates (starches and bigger sugars) in food. Oxygen combines with glucose and, with the help of other chemicals, breaks down the glucose to release its energy. This energy is essential for powering the processes of living, growing and moving.

Keeping living things alive

Nearly all living things need oxygen to survive. They include plants from seaweeds to trees, animals from worms to whales, fungi such as mushrooms, and microscopic organisms like amoebas and bacteria. Since oxygen cannot be stored long-term, all these living things need fresh supplies continuously. Only a few microbes can live without oxygen, in oxygen-less places such as the mud at the bottom of the sea.

Since you are a living thing, you need oxygen to survive. You get it by breathing fresh air into your lungs, absorbing some of the oxygen from it, and breathing out the stale air: a process called respiration. As described on the next few pages, the oxygen passes from the air spaces in the lungs, into the blood flowing around these air spaces, through an intricate network of blood vessels. The blood continues to flow around the body, pumped by the heart, and carries the oxygen to every part. If a part of the body is deprived of oxygen for more than a few minutes, it begins to die.

the respiratory system

The parts of the body involved in passing oxygen from the air into the bloodstream are known as the respiratory system. Air can flow through the nose or mouth. The nose is designed to prepare air for the lungs by warming it, moistening it and filtering bits of dust from it with the nasal hairs and nasal mucus.

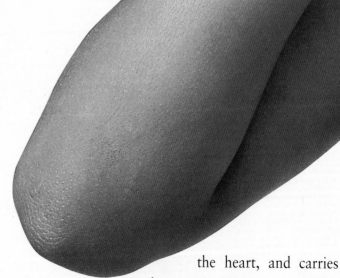

useful airflow

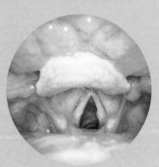

As air flows out of the lungs, we can use it to make the sounds of speech and other noises. At the top of the windpipe, in the sides of the voicebox or larynx, are two stiff, shelf-like folds – called the vocal cords. Criss-crossed muscles in the voice-box can pull these together (left, above) so that air passes through a narrow slit between them and makes them vibrate, creating sounds. As the vocal cords are pulled tighter, they make higher-pitched sounds. As the vocal cords loosen, they make lower-pitched sounds. In normal breathing the vocal cords are far apart (left, below) and air flows silently through the wide gap between them.

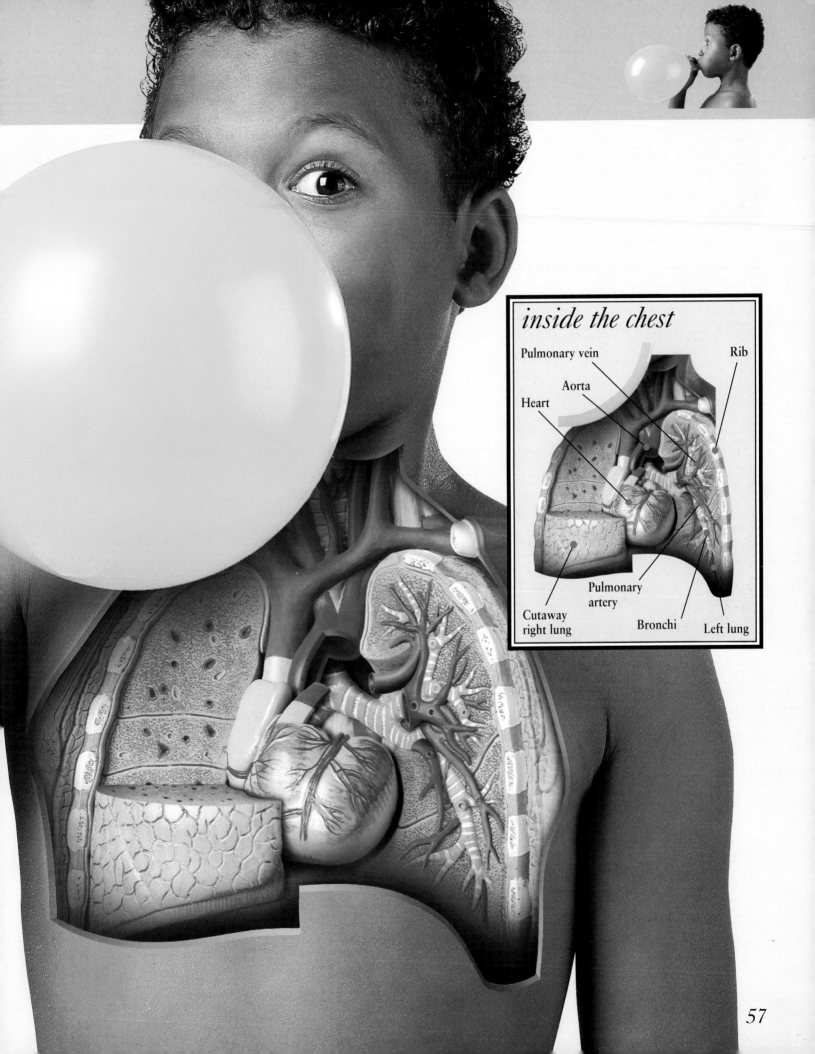

inside the chest

Pulmonary vein

Aorta

Heart

Rib

Cutaway
right lung

Pulmonary
artery

Bronchi

Left lung

deep in the lungs

LIKE ALL MOVEMENTS IN THE BODY, those of breathing rely on muscle power (see page 38). There are two main sets of breathing muscles: the intercostal muscles and the diaphragm. The intercostal muscles are shaped like straps and sit between each pair of ribs. As they contract, they pull the ribs closer together. This makes the whole ribcage swing upwards and outwards. Breathe in deeply and watch your ribs rise and your chest expand.
The diaphragm is a curved sheet of muscle at the base of the chest, forming a roof over the liver, stomach, the intestines and other parts in the abdomen below it. As the diaphragm contracts, it changes from an upwardly curved, dome shape (like an upturned bowl) to a flatter, plate shape. This has the effect of pulling down the curved bases of the lungs, which are situated just above the diaphragm, and increasing them in size.

dirt and damage

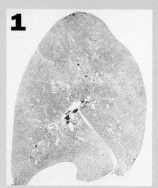

The delicate alveoli inside the lungs can be damaged by many things. One is tobacco smoke, which clogs the alveoli and airways with thick tar. Others are the polluting gases that hover in the air of many big cities, coming from vehicle exhausts as well as factory and power-station chimneys. Some types of industrial dust and particles floating in the air, such as asbestos or

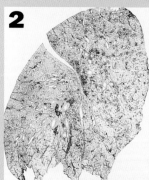

coal-mine dust, can also harm the lungs. Some of these particles cause changes in the cells making up the lungs. The cells begin to multiply out of control. This is one type of lung cancer. A slice of healthy lung is shown above (1), to compare with a city dweller's polluted lung (2).

How you breathe

Together, these muscles make the chest bigger and stretch the spongy lungs inside. As the lungs enlarge, they suck in air down the windpipe. This is how you breathe in. Then the muscles relax. The ribs fall back down and the diaphragm resumes its domed shape as the spongy, elastic lungs spring back to their smaller size. The lungs blow some of their air up the windpipe. This is how you breathe out.

The movements of breathing are controlled by the brain. Its "automatic pilot" (see page 102) sends out signals to make the muscles contract. The signals pass along nerves to the intercostal and diaphragm muscles, making them contract. This happens every few seconds throughout your life, even when you are asleep. If you are exercising heavily and need lots more oxygen, other muscles help with breathing, such as those in the shoulders, back and abdomen.

Air flowing down the windpipe passes into the main tube, or bronchus, to each lung. This tube splits into smaller ones, which divide again into

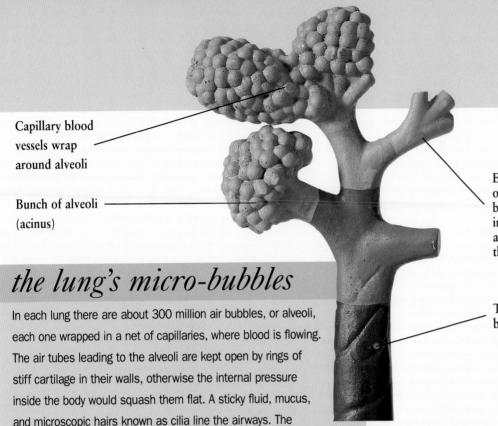

Capillary blood
vessels wrap
around alveoli

Bunch of alveoli
(acinus)

Each branch
of terminal
bronchiole ends
in a bunch of
alveoli, called
the acinus

Terminal
bronchiole

the lung's micro-bubbles

In each lung there are about 300 million air bubbles, or alveoli, each one wrapped in a net of capillaries, where blood is flowing. The air tubes leading to the alveoli are kept open by rings of stiff cartilage in their walls, otherwise the internal pressure inside the body would squash them flat. A sticky fluid, mucus, and microscopic hairs known as cilia line the airways. The mucus traps dirt and dust, and the cilia wave to and fro to sweep the dirty mucus up and out of the lungs. This keeps the lungs clean.

even smaller ones. Deep inside the lungs, the air tubes are as thin as hairs, and are called terminal bronchioles. They end at groups of microscopic "air bubbles" known as alveoli, like hollow grapes on a stalk. Each alveolus has a network of tiny blood vessels – capillaries – wrapped around it. Oxygen from the air passes through the alveolus lining into the blood in the capillaries, which carries it around the body.

Two-way traffic

Breathing is not a one-way process of taking in oxygen. Cellular respiration makes a waste product – carbon dioxide. If this built up in cells, it would poison them. So carbon dioxide is collected around the body and taken away by the blood that has just deposited its oxygen. As this blood flows back through the lungs, carbon dioxide passes through the alveolus lining to the air on the other side. This means that gases are moving to and from the air into the blood. The effect is that in the lungs, oxygen moves from air to blood, and carbon dioxide moves from blood to air. Then you breathe out, getting rid of the stale lower-oxygen air, ready to take in fresh air with the next breath.

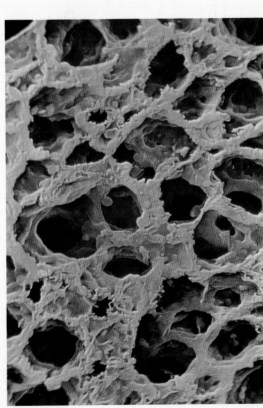

*This microscope photograph shows
the cut-through alveoli in the lungs.*

round and round...

THE DIGESTIVE SYSTEM gets energy-rich nutrients, especially glucose sugars, into the body. The respiratory system gets oxygen into the body. These two substances are combined in cells, by the chemical process of cellular respiration, to provide the energy that powers life. But how do oxygen, sugars and other nutrients reach every cell in the body?

The answer is via the two circulatory systems. The main one is the cardiovascular system. This consists of the fluid "transport medium" called blood, flowing through tubes known as blood vessels (vascular tubes), pumped by the heart (the cardiac pump). This system is described in detail on the following pages.

The lymphatic system

The second, less familiar, circulatory system is the lymphatic system. This also has a fluid – the pale, milky or straw-coloured lymph. It also flows along tubes, known as lymph vessels. However, it moves much more sluggishly than blood, since it does not have its own pump. The lymph is pushed along by indirect pressure, from the pulsing of the blood vessels and by the massaging effects of body movements.

The lymphatic system has no clear beginning. Lymph starts as the general body fluids which collect around and between cells. It flows slowly into the larger lymph vessels. These join into the biggest lymph tubes, or ducts, in the chest and abdomen. These connect with large blood vessels and so empty the lymph fluid into the main blood circulation. The lymphatic system ends, as lymph merges with blood.

Lymph carries small amounts of oxygen around the body. It also transports nutrients, especially fats, which it absorbs into vessels called lacteals, in the lining of the small intestine. Lymph collects waste products, too, from cells all over the body. In these jobs it is far less important than blood.

However, in another job, lymph is extremely important. It carries the white cells that fight disease and any germs that get into the body. The white cells collect in widened parts of lymph vessels which are called lymph nodes, or sometimes "glands". As the body combats an illness, the lymph nodes get bigger with extra white cells and their germ-killing chemicals, as well as dead and dying germs and increased amounts of body fluids. We call the enlarged lymph nodes "swollen glands". The body's battle against germs is described in more detail on page 80. Various diseases such as lymphomas and leukaemias can affect the lymph system and the white blood cells it contains.

described in more detail on page 80.

two circulations

The blood system reaches all parts of the body. The lymph system is concentrated mainly in the neck, body, shoulders and hips. Each system helps to distribute nutrients around the body and to collect wastes for disposal. Lymph fluid rejoins the blood via the thoracic duct and other main lymph ducts. The thymus in the neck, and the spleen behind the stomach, have an especially rich supply of lymph.

inside a lymph node

There are groups of lymph nodes, or "glands", in the neck, armpits, chest, abdomen and groin. Valves in the lymph vessels make sure that the lymph fluid flows the correct way through each node. Inside the lymph node are clumps of disease-fighting and waste-removing cells. Like all other organs, the lymph node receives its own blood supply.

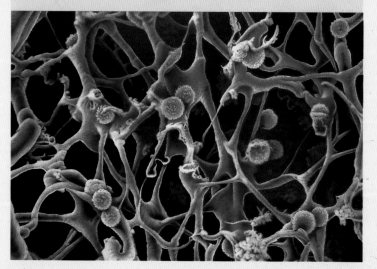

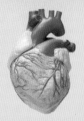

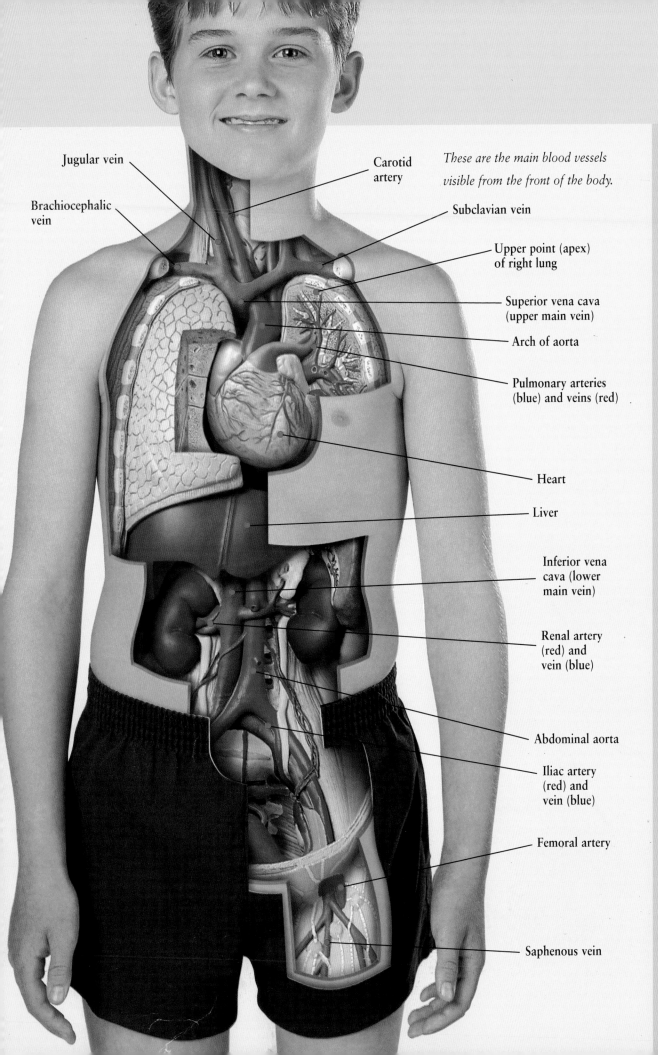

Jugular vein

Brachiocephalic vein

Carotid artery

These are the main blood vessels visible from the front of the body.

Subclavian vein

Upper point (apex) of right lung

Superior vena cava (upper main vein)

Arch of aorta

Pulmonary arteries (blue) and veins (red)

Heart

Liver

Inferior vena cava (lower main vein)

Renal artery (red) and vein (blue)

Abdominal aorta

Iliac artery (red) and vein (blue)

Femoral artery

Saphenous vein

did you know?

➤ AN AVERAGE PERSON HAS ABOUT 400–450 LYMPH NODES.

➤ THE LARGEST NODES ARE AS BIG AS WALNUTS.

➤ DURING AN ILLNESS, THEY CAN SWELL TO BECOME BIGGER THAN TENNIS BALLS.

➤ THE SMALLEST LYMPH NODES ARE TINIER THAN RICE GRAINS.

➤ THERE IS BETWEEN 1 AND 2 LITRES (2–4 PINTS) OF LYMPH FLUID IN A TYPICAL HUMAN BODY.

➤ AN AVERAGE LYMPH NODE MAKES ABOUT 10 BILLION OF THE WHITE BLOOD CELLS CALLED LYMPHOCYTES, EACH DAY.

➤ LYMPH FLOWS UP TO 15 TIMES FASTER DURING VIGOROUS ACTIVITY THAN IT DOES AT REST.

➤ THE TONSILS ARE LUMPS OF LYMPH TISSUE.

the vital beat

LUB-DUB, LUB-DUB... This is the sound of the heartbeat, a noise that signals life. Actually, it's the sound of the non-return valves inside the heart, slapping open and closed with each beat. The valves ensure that blood flows properly in one direction only through the heart and then around the body's system of blood vessels. Without the valves, blood might simply splosh to and fro inside the heart and blood vessels, like the tide going in and out, and never circulate at all.

The heart's valves are made of soft, flexible tissue, like rubbery leather. The rest of the heart is a blood-filled bag of muscle. Every second or so the muscle contracts and squeezes the blood out into main blood vessels called arteries. Then it relaxes and the bag refills with more blood, which flows in from main vessels called veins. In fact, the heart is really two bags of muscle joined down one side – two pumps side by side. The valves divide each side of the heart into two chambers. The upper, smaller chamber is the atrium, which receives blood flowing in from the main veins. The larger, lower chamber is the ventricle. It has very thick walls, receives blood through the valve from the atrium above, and provides the main pumping power as it squeezes the blood out through another valve into the main arteries.

inside the heart

The heart is divided into two parts by the central wall, called the septum. Each part is divided into two chambers by a large, flexible, funnel-shaped valve. The heart nestles between the two spongy lungs, in a hollow formed by the scooped-out shape of the left lung. The powerful writhing movements of each beat are lubricated by a smooth, slippery bag around it – the pericardium. The heart muscle has its own blood supply, from the coronary arteries and veins over its surface.

stages in a heartbeat

There are four stages to a heartbeat. They merge smoothly into each other and into the next beat. The speed of beating is controlled by nerve signals from the brain and by chemicals called hormones circulating in the blood.

1 The heart relaxes and refills in the phase of its beat called diastole (die-ass-tow-lee). Blood flows into the two atria from the main veins.

2 The thin but muscular walls of the atria contract, propelling blood through the main valves into the ventricles.

3 The ventricles contract strongly, in the phase of the heartbeat called systole (sis-tow-lee). Blood inside them is squeezed hard.

4 The blood in the ventricles is forced through more non-return valves into the main arteries, and out to the body and lungs.

How your heart beats

The pump on the right side of the heart (on the left as you look at someone) receives blood that has been pumped around the body. This blood is dark red and has used up most of its oxygen (shown in blue

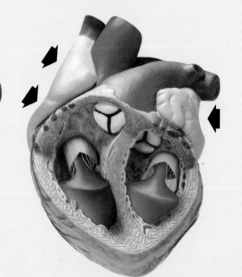

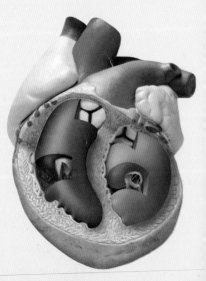

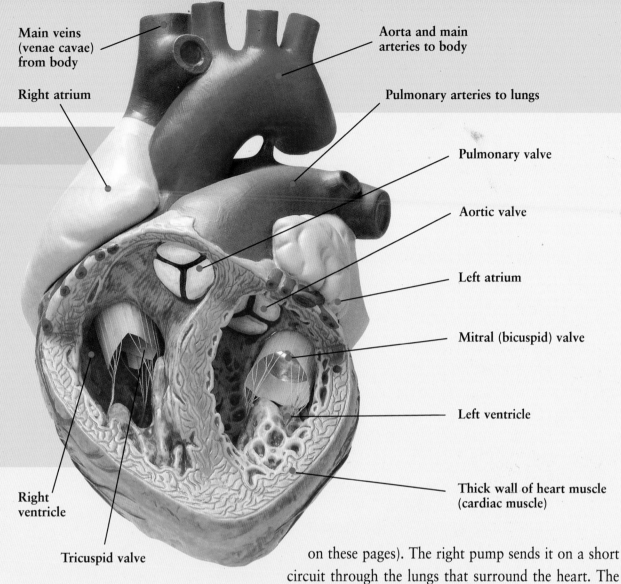

Main veins (venae cavae) from body

Right atrium

Aorta and main arteries to body

Pulmonary arteries to lungs

Pulmonary valve

Aortic valve

Left atrium

Mitral (bicuspid) valve

Left ventricle

Thick wall of heart muscle (cardiac muscle)

Right ventricle

Tricuspid valve

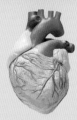

did you know?

➤ THE HEART OF AN AVERAGE PERSON AT REST BEATS 60–80 TIMES EACH MINUTE.

➤ EACH BEAT SENDS ABOUT 70 ml (0.14 pt) OF BLOOD OUT OF EACH VENTRICLE.

➤ THIS MEANS THAT, AT REST, THE HEART PUMPS SOME 5–6 l (1.25–1.3 gal) OF BLOOD EACH MINUTE.

➤ IF THE BODY IS VERY ACTIVE, THE MUSCLES NEED MORE ENERGY AND OXYGEN SO THE HEART MAY BEAT UP TO 200 TIMES EACH MINUTE.

➤ THE HEART CAN ALSO INCREASE THE BLOOD IT PUMPS WITH EACH BEAT – UP TO 200 ml (0.4 pt).

➤ SO WHEN THE BODY IS VERY ACTIVE, THE HEART CAN PUMP 40 l (9 gall) OF BLOOD EACH MINUTE. THAT WOULD FILL A BATHTUB IN TWO MINUTES.

on these pages). The right pump sends it on a short circuit through the lungs that surround the heart. The blood comes back bright red and rich in oxygen, to the heart's left side, ready for its journey around the body. The heart's left-side pump is larger and more powerful than the right side because it has to send blood out under great pressure, to flow all around the body. When the heart stops beating, body tissues no longer receive fresh blood, carrying oxygen and nutrients. So life ends. However, in hospital, the cardiopulmonary machine can take over the job of heart and lungs. This means doctors can resuscitate people or carry out operations on the heart, such as replacing diseased valves.

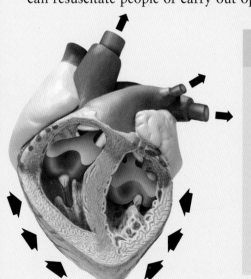

spare-part heart

Sometimes the heart valves become stiff or leaky. They can be replaced by valves made from tissue taken from an animal, or by artificial valves made of metal and plastic. The small coronary blood vessels supplying the heart's own muscle may get blocked. They can be bypassed by using "spare" vessels taken from the legs, as shown here.

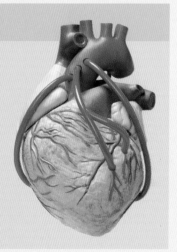

63

highways and byways

THE ONLY LIVING PARTS of your body that do not have blood vessels are the lens and cornea, the transparent bits at the front of your eye. The rest of the body has an amazingly complex and delicate system of blood vessels, carrying the blood to every nook and cranny, and then returning it to the heart. If all these blood vessels could be linked, they would stretch halfway to the moon. The blood vessels act like a road network. There are two major kinds of "main road" – arteries and veins.

The arteries carry blood away from the heart. They have thick, strong, muscular walls to stand up to the high-pressure surge of blood, which spurts out of the heart on each beat. The artery walls balloon out slightly with the pressure. You can feel this pulsing surge in the artery in your wrist, the radial artery. We call this surge "the pulse". There is one pulsation for each heartbeat so the pulse and heartbeat rates are the same.

arteries and veins

Long arteries in the arm carry blood towards the hand, and also supply smaller branches along the way. Veins do the reverse, collecting blood for returning to the heart. These vessels are tough and good at preventing kinking as the arm moves.

The brachial artery branches farther down

Brachial artery

Basilic vein

Humerus

Venule   Arteriole

arterioles and venules

Small arterioles and venules form an immense network servicing almost every body part. In some places they run alongside each other, as shown here in one of the tiny blob-like units in the liver, called a liver lobule. But in most places they form a more random, branching pattern, as in the guts and muscles.

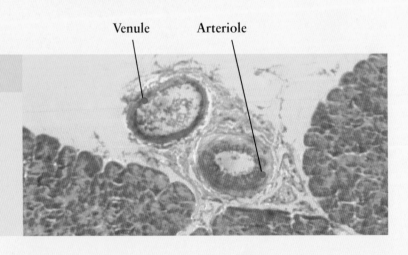

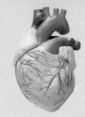

The usual, convenient, place to feel "the pulse" is in the radial artery in the wrist, just over the radius forearm bone.

Radial artery
where you can feel your pulse

Ulnar artery

Branching out

As main roads divide into smaller roads, so the arteries branch and divide into smaller tubes – arterioles. The branching process continues until the tubes are thinner than hairs and can be seen only under a microscope. They are now called capillaries. A capillary has an incredibly thin wall, only one cell thick. Oxygen, nutrients and other substances can diffuse easily from the blood inside the capillary, through the thin wall, to the surrounding cells and tissues. At the same time wastes seep the other way, from cells and tissues into the blood, and are carried away.

The capillaries join together to make larger tubes – venules. These come together into even wider tubes – veins. By now the blood has lost its high-pressure surge from each heartbeat. It oozes along slowly so the veins need only thin, floppy walls. On average, it takes a drop of blood about one minute to go from the heart, out into an artery, along an arteriole until it reaches a capillary, where it delivers its supplies of oxygen, nutrients and other substances such as hormones (see page 108), and then into a venule and along a vein, back to the heart. Of course, there is great variation. A round trip to the stomach takes a few seconds since it is so near the heart, while a journey all the way down to the toes and back takes much longer.

capillaries

A typical capillary is so thin that it can only be seen under a microscope. It is also just 1–2 mm long. Blood spends only about one-tenth of a second in a capillary. But millions of them form a vast area where blood can pass nutrients, oxygen and other substances to cells.

Branching capillary

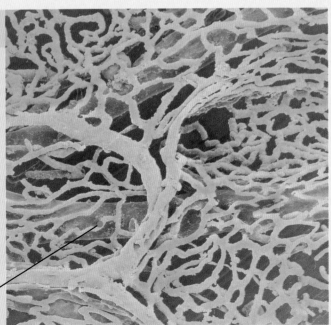

warm, red and sticky

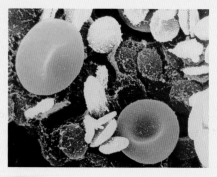

Blood contains a mixture of red, white and other cells.

BLOOD IS ONE OF THE MOST COMPLICATED fluids known: it does dozens of jobs and contains hundreds of substances. Fresh blood flowing around the body is a sign of health. Blood spurting from a cut or unable to get through a blocked vessel is a sign of danger. Blood is so important to life that it is mentioned on most of the pages in this book; these pages tell you more about it.

Blood carries oxygen, which it picks up in the lungs. It distributes this oxygen to all body parts, since every body cell needs a regular supply of oxygen to stay alive, as described on page 56. The oxygen is carried around stuck to a substance called haemoglobin, a body protein. Some 250 million molecules of haemoglobin are packaged into one doughnut-shaped red blood cell. There are five million red blood cells in each tiny pinprick of blood.

Collecting wastes for disposal

Blood also carries sugars, minerals and nutrients around the body, which have come from either digested food or the body's nutrient stores in fat and in the liver. In addition, blood collects wastes from the life processes of the body cells. A main waste is carbon dioxide, produced when sugars are broken down for their energy. Carbon dioxide is absorbed from cells and tissues into the blood, and then passes into the air inside the lungs and is breathed out, as explained on page 59.

Fighting disease

An important job for blood is to fight disease. As well as red blood cells, blood contains another main type of cell, the white blood cell. In fact there are many kinds of white cell, such as lymphocytes, macrophages and neutrophils. The general task of the white blood cells is to battle against invaders and foreign objects that might get into your body when you breathe or eat, or through a cut in your skin. These white cells are part of the immune defence system, as shown on page 80.

blood transfusions

Like muscle or bone, blood is one of the body's tissues. It can be transplanted from one person to another, too – by what we call a blood transfusion. However, different people have different kinds, or groups, of blood. If the wrong groups are mixed together, the result can be serious blood clots. So the medical staff must check the blood group of a person before a small amount of their blood is donated and before it is transfused into another person. The donated blood may be kept cool and used whole. Or it may be separated into its various components, which are kept in cold storage and have different "shelf lives".

white blood cells

A typical white blood cell is not white but almost colourless or transparent. It can change shape, push out folds and finger-like projections, and move along by oozing and crawling, like an amoeba in a pond. The general name for white blood cells is leucocytes. Some are not in the blood at all. They squeeze between the cells which form capillary walls, and slide off into the surrounding tissues, to hunt invaders and scavenge debris.

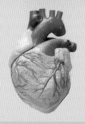

red blood cells

The doughnut shape of the erythrocyte has a large surface area compared to the volume of its interior, in order to absorb as much oxygen as possible. It's a small bag-like cell, only 7 micrometres (0.007 mm) across, that can change shape to squeeze though the narrowest capillaries. And it is "degenerate" as it contains almost nothing but haemoglobin. The normal cell inner parts, like the nucleus and mitochondria, break down during the cell's development.

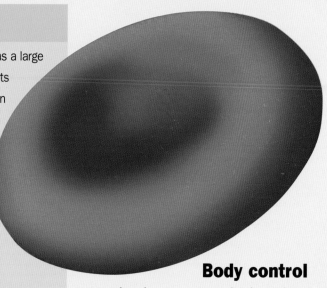

Body control

Blood contains body chemicals called hormones. These control and coordinate many body processes, such as growing, using energy, sexual developments, and adjusting the amounts of water and minerals in the body – see page 108.

And blood is warm. It works like the liquid in a central heating system. It absorbs warmth from busy parts such as the heart and muscles, and spreads this out to cooler parts, like the skin. This helps to keep the whole body at much the same temperature, as described on page 78. When it leaks out of the body, blood goes sticky and forms a lump to seal leaks, cuts and wounds. We call this blood-clotting, and it's described on page 82. Blood's distribution around the body is controlled by muscle layers in the artery walls. If they contract, the artery becomes narrower and less blood flows to the organ it supplies. During exercise, for example, the body's muscles receive ten times the amount of blood (12 litres per minute) than at rest.

blood in a capillary

An average adult body has about 5 litres (1.25 gall) – 5,000 ml (10 pints) – of blood. At any one moment, about 1,250 ml (2.5 pints) are in the arteries, 3,500 ml (7 pints) in the veins, and 250 ml (0.5 pints) in the capillaries. A typical capillary is so narrow that the microscopic blood cells have to line up in single file to pass through it. The red blood cells shown here are packed into a slightly larger capillary. The cells in blood are only flowing through a capillary for half a second before they move into the next type of vessels, small veins.

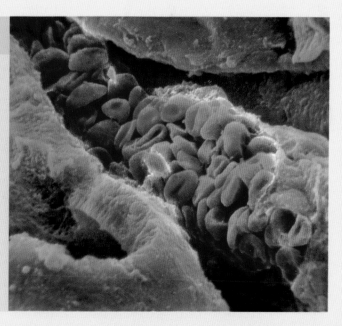

did you know?

BLOOD HAS FOUR MAIN PARTS, OR COMPONENTS:

▶ ALMOST ONE-HALF CONSISTS OF RED CELLS, CALLED ERYTHROCYTES, THAT CARRY OXYGEN AND CARBON DIOXIDE.

▶ A MUCH SMALLER PROPORTION IS MADE UP OF WHITE CELLS. THEY FIGHT INVADERS AND DISEASE, AND CLEAN THE BLOOD OF DEBRIS AND UNWANTED MATERIAL.

▶ A TINY FRACTION CONSISTS OF PLATELETS. THESE ARE NOT WHOLE CELLS BUT PARTS OR FRAGMENTS OF CELLS. THEY HELP BLOOD TO CLOT.

▶ JUST OVER HALF OF BLOOD IS PLASMA, A PALE YELLOW, SWEET-SMELLING, STICKY FLUID. IT CONTAINS HUNDREDS OF DISSOLVED SUBSTANCES, FROM SUGARS FOR ENERGY, TO HORMONES, TO WASTES LIKE CARBON DIOXIDE.

chapter

4

keeping constant

WHEN YOU ARE in a very hot and humid place, such as in a tropical country during a heat wave, it is a great relief to get into an air-conditioned room. Similarly, if you are outside on a cold day without enough thick clothes, you are glad to get into a warm room. The body is not comfortable in places that are too hot or too cold, or too dry or too humid. It works best in certain steady, stable conditions.

The same is true of the cells inside the body. They work best in certain conditions, such as when they are in a constant temperature and are

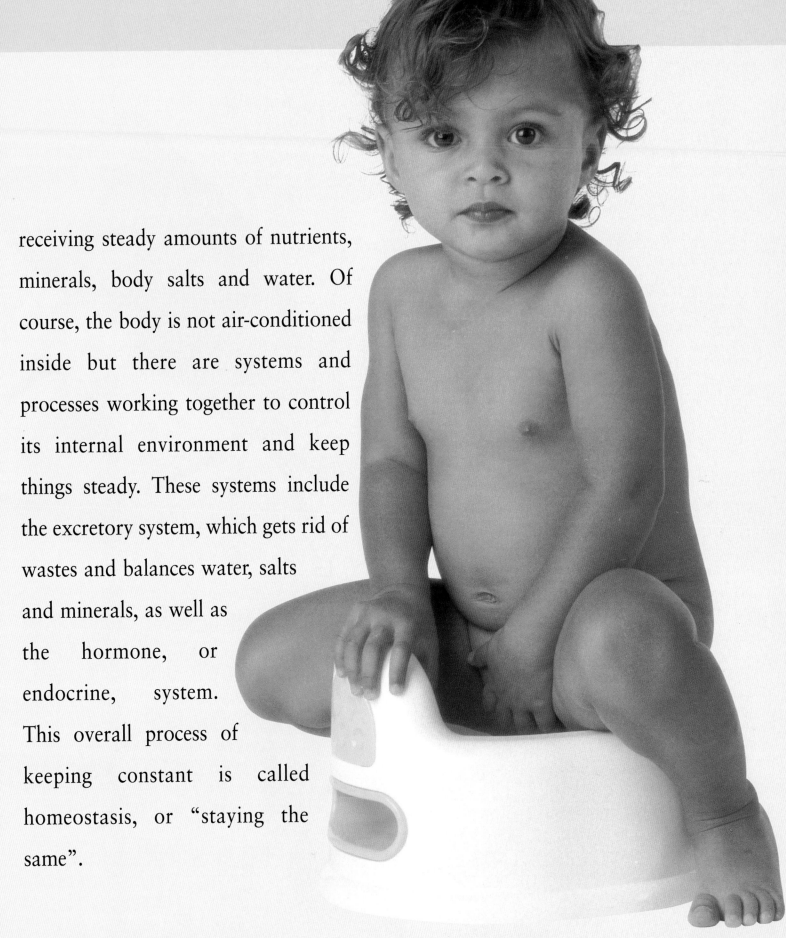

receiving steady amounts of nutrients, minerals, body salts and water. Of course, the body is not air-conditioned inside but there are systems and processes working together to control its internal environment and keep things steady. These systems include the excretory system, which gets rid of wastes and balances water, salts and minerals, as well as the hormone, or endocrine, system. This overall process of keeping constant is called homeostasis, or "staying the same".

steady as you go

THE BODY IS LIKE A VERY INTRICATE MACHINE with millions of working parts. A real machine that is very delicate and complicated needs to be cared for and kept in constant conditions. If it gets too cold or too hot, its parts start to seize up. The same happens with the body, also in a chemical way, not just in a mechanical way. The body's thousands of chemical life processes need fairly constant conditions or they go wrong, and the result is discomfort, ill health or even death.

Stable conditions

The name for this "constancy of the internal environment" is homeostasis. The body must regulate many systems and processes to keep inner conditions stable. Homeostatic processes are always coming into action. If you run fast suddenly, your muscles use up lots of blood sugar (glucose) and oxygen, and make lots of heat and carbon dioxide. Outside, you can see that you breathe faster and harder, to take in more oxygen and get rid of the carbon dioxide. Inside your body, the liver changes its stores of starch into sugar and releases these into the blood, to restore the normal level of blood sugar. All the time, even as you sleep, hundreds of these detailed adjustments are happening inside you.

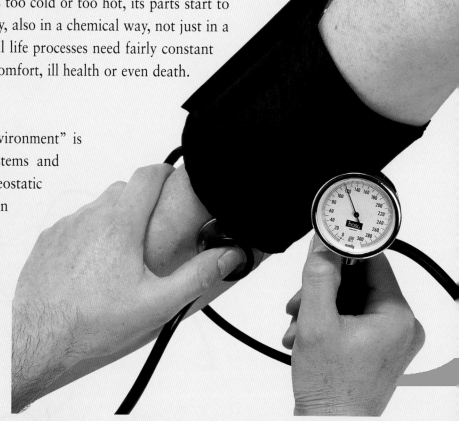

Blood pressure is usually measured with an inflatable cuff around the upper arm.

Body variables

Conditions that can vary are called variables. In the body, there are hundreds of them. One is body temperature. This tries to go up when we rush about and get excited, and if the weather is very hot. It tries to go down when we are inactive, or when it is cold. But homeostatic processes such as sweating and flushing or shivering, keep our temperature constant (see page 78). The central (or core) temperature rarely varies by more than one degree from the normal 37 °C (98.6 °F).

Another variable is blood pressure, which is the pushing strength of blood mainly on the walls of its arteries as it surges through them after a heartbeat. If

staying cool and calm

Through the day, the body rests and then moves at different speeds, has a meal and then does not eat, takes a drink and then does not drink. Sometimes people get so excited that they shout and leap around; when they are sleeping they may hardly move at all. Despite these variations, the body's inner conditions are designed to stay much the same.

70

body control

Movement and excitement, especially in sports, tend to raise the body's inner, or core, temperature. Homeostatic processes work to reduce it back to normal. These are controlled by the nervous and hormonal systems, and they include sweating, flushing and breathing faster, to get rid of excess warmth. Even body movements can be homeostatic. A hot person may spread out arms and legs to increase heat loss, a cold person curls up to reduce the areas of the body losing warmth.

this becomes too high, it can put too much strain on the heart and blood vessels, and cause illness.

There are many important chemicals and minerals in the body, from oxygen, carbon dioxide and blood sugar (glucose), to calcium, iron, sodium, potassium and chloride. These are also variables. Each is controlled by homeostatic processes, so that it stays within healthy limits. For example, too much blood sugar may lead to the condition known as diabetes. If not treated by eating certain foods, taking tablets or having injections of the controlling hormone insulin, it can cause serious illness and even death.

helping homeostasis

The kidneys play a vital role in filtering the blood, to remove wastes and excess salts and minerals. If they cannot work properly, perhaps due to infection or disease, then wastes build up in the blood. This can be very serious. In dialysis, a person's blood is led along tubes through a dialyser, or "artificial kidney", and back into the body. The dialyser filters it and removes most of the wastes.

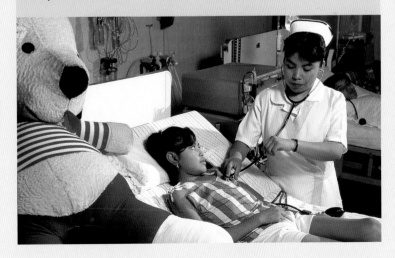

71

waste disposal

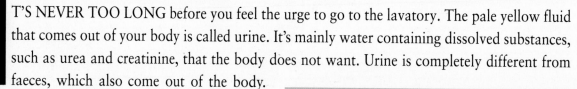

I T'S NEVER TOO LONG before you feel the urge to go to the lavatory. The pale yellow fluid that comes out of your body is called urine. It's mainly water containing dissolved substances, such as urea and creatinine, that the body does not want. Urine is completely different from faeces, which also come out of the body. Urine is wastes filtered from the blood by the kidneys. Faeces are leftovers from digestion in the intestines. Getting rid of something that the body no longer needs is called excretion. Urine and faeces are both products of excretion. So is breathing out carbon dioxide. So is sweating, since sweat contains certain chemicals and salts, including some substances that give the distinctive smells to certain foods, such as garlic.

the excretory system

The main parts of the excretory system are in the abdomen. They are the two kidneys, on either side just under the liver and stomach, and the bladder, lower down in middle at the front. A tube called a ureter carries urine from each kidney to the bladder. Another tube, the urethra, carries it from the bladder to the outside.

Kidney balancing act

The kidneys don't just filter the blood to make urine, as described overleaf. They also adjust the amounts and balance of various body chemicals, and of water itself. If a person drinks, it is absorbed by the digestive system into the blood. Too much water in the blood makes it weaker, or more dilute. So the levels, or concentrations, of blood chemicals go down. This is a job for homeostasis!

As the blood becomes more dilute and watery, this is detected by a tiny sensor in the part of the brain called the hypothalamus. The hypothalamus passes the information to a tiny gland just under the brain – the pituitary gland (see page 109). The pituitary responds by releasing smaller amounts of a hormone chemical called ADH (anti-diuretic hormone). ADH circulates in the blood to all body parts, including the kidneys. The kidneys react to this fall in blood ADH by adjusting their filtering of the blood to get rid of more water than usual from it. And so the blood becomes less weak and watery, and gets back to normal. As it does so, the amount of ADH gradually rises.

There are dozens of similar body hormones and control processes. Many of them are linked together and affect each other. For example, as blood takes in water and becomes weaker, its volume goes up. This makes blood pressure rise, so more hormones are released to control it, along with the brain's nerve signals.

water in	water out
Made by chemical processes in the body (metabolic water) – 300 ml (0.6 pints)	Sweating (average climate) – 200 ml (0.4 pints)
	In "solid" wastes or faeces – 200 ml (0.4 pints)
In food – 600 ml (1.2 pints)	Vapour from lungs – 400 ml (0.8 pints)
	Evaporating from skin – 400 ml (0.8 pints)
In drinks – 1,500 ml (3 pints)	In urine – 1,200 ml (2.4 pints)
Total 2,400 ml (4.8 pints)	Total 2,400 ml (4.8 pints) per day

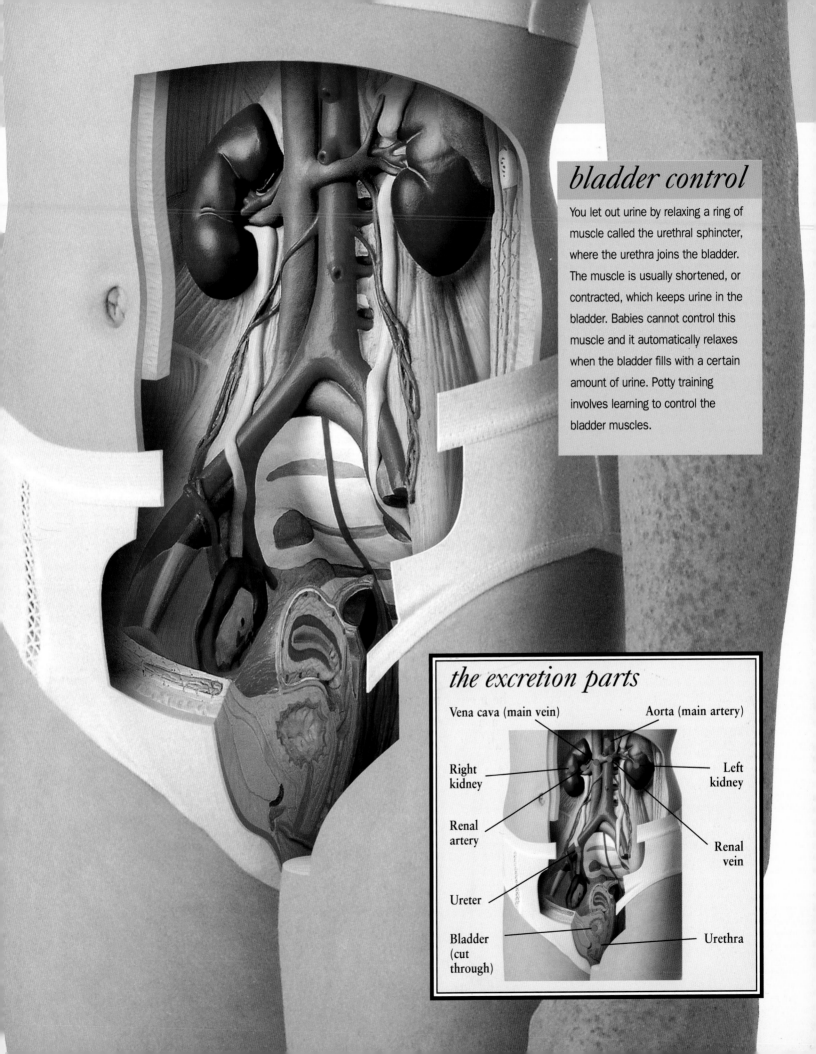

bladder control

You let out urine by relaxing a ring of muscle called the urethral sphincter, where the urethra joins the bladder. The muscle is usually shortened, or contracted, which keeps urine in the bladder. Babies cannot control this muscle and it automatically relaxes when the bladder fills with a certain amount of urine. Potty training involves learning to control the bladder muscles.

the excretion parts

Vena cava (main vein)

Aorta (main artery)

Right kidney

Left kidney

Renal artery

Renal vein

Ureter

Bladder (cut through)

Urethra

incredible bio-filters

THE KIDNEYS ARE TWO of the body's most remarkable organs. For each person they are about the size of their cupped hand. There is one each side, towards the back of the abdomen, on either side of the backbone. The tops of the kidneys are protected by the lower ribs. The bulging liver on the right-hand side means that the right kidney is slightly lower than the left one.

The kidneys get a plentiful blood supply – about 70 l (17.5 galls) every hour. This means that the body's blood passes through them 400 times every day. The blood comes along the wide renal artery, and very slightly less blood goes back along the renal vein. This is because the kidney's main job is to sieve the blood through microscopic filtering units called nephrons, and to collect the wastes and unwanted substances from it to make urine. There are about one million nephrons in each kidney.

How the kidneys work

Inside the kidney there are two main layers – the outer cortex and the inner medulla. In the centre is the renal pelvis, a bumpy-walled cavity where urine collects then trickles away down the ureter to the bladder. When blood arrives in the kidney, it flows into part of each nephron called the glomerulus. This is a tiny knot of microscopic capillaries. There are a million or so glomeruli packed into the kidney's cortex. Water and some chemicals are squeezed out of the capillaries, into a cup-shaped part around it called the Bowman's capsule. Useful things like blood cells are too big to get squeezed out of the capillaries.

kidney stones

If the kidney does not work properly, the space in the renal pelvis may get "furred up" like a kettle, with hard crusts and crystals of chemicals from the urine. These are kidney stones, or renal calculi. They can be removed by an operation, dissolved by medical drugs, or shattered into tiny fragments by high-energy ultrasonic sound waves.

inside the kidney

The kidney's outer layer (1), called the cortex, is made up mostly of the million or so knots of capillaries, the glomeruli, with a Bowman's capsule (2) around each one. The medulla consists mainly of the long loops of U-shaped renal tubules, and the collecting ducts for urine. On top of each kidney is the adrenal gland, also called the supra-renal gland, which makes various hormones.

Bowman's capsule

Urine collecting duct

Renal tubule

Cortex

Medulla

1

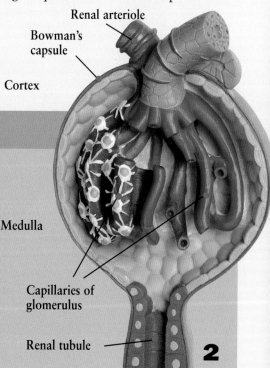

Renal arteriole

Bowman's capsule

Capillaries of glomerulus

Renal tubule

2

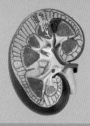

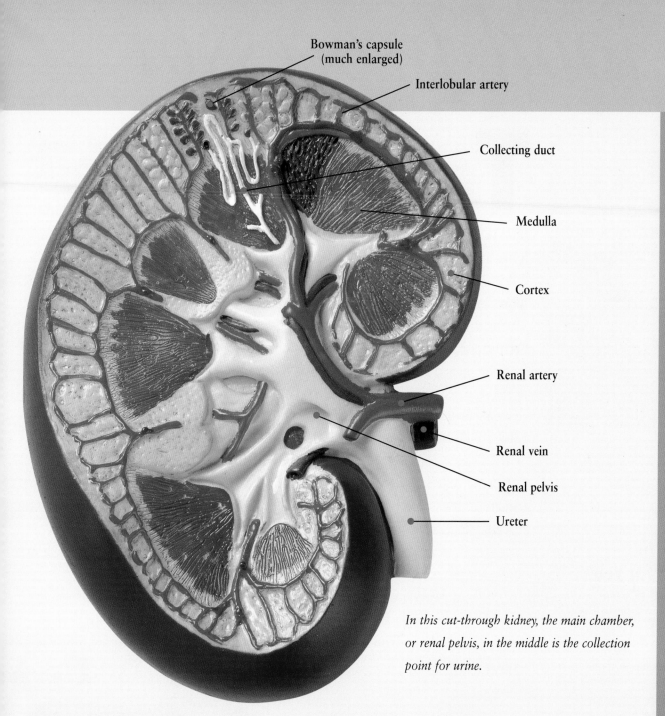

Bowman's capsule
(much enlarged)

Interlobular artery

Collecting duct

Medulla

Cortex

Renal artery

Renal vein

Renal pelvis

Ureter

*In this cut-through kidney, the main chamber,
or renal pelvis, in the middle is the collection
point for urine.*

How urine is made

The water-and-chemical mixture dribbles slowly through the next part of the nephron – a long but microscopic U-shaped pipe – the renal tubule. This dips down into the kidney's medulla, then back up into the cortex. It is surrounded by more capillaries. Useful substances such as glucose and much of the water pass from the renal tubule back into the blood. This leaves a strong, concentrated solution of water plus unwanted substances, mainly urea. This is urine. It trickles from the tubule, along larger and larger tubes, into the kidney's pelvis. Then it flows along the ureter, a muscular tube, to the urinary bladder. This is a stretchy, muscle-walled bag that swells like a balloon as it fills.

The kidneys are incredibly efficient. Every minute about 120 ml (0.24 pints) of water and chemicals pass from the blood into their tubules. Yet so much water and useful substances are taken back from the tubules into the blood that only 1 ml (0.002 pints) of this is left as urine. The rates of blood flow, filtering and urine production slow greatly during sleep.

the food processor

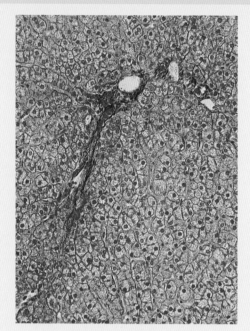

Under the microscope, liver cells can be seen in layers and sheets that form a sponge-like structure. The holes are blood vessels.

THE LIVER IS ONE OF THE BODY'S busiest parts. It does not squirm about or move, like the stomach, intestines, heart or muscles. Its activities are invisible – at the chemical level. The liver is the body's largest inner organ, weighing around 1.2–1.6 kg (2lb 9 oz–3lb 8 oz), and fills the top part of the abdomen, especially on the right side.

It has at least 500 known jobs in body chemistry, all different and important. There are probably more liver processes waiting to be discovered. The liver has a special blood vessel to it – the hepatic portal vein. This does not come directly from the heart, but carries blood that has been to the stomach, intestines and spleen. This blood is rich in nutrients, which provide the body with its energy and raw materials. It seeps through the main part of the liver, which is made of thousands of tiny six-sided groups of cells known as hepatic lobules. Each resembles a miniature honeycomb. Most of the cells are hepatocytes, specialized to carry out dozens of intricate chemical processes.

Left lobe

Liver is good for you

The liver processes, in various ways, many of the nutrients brought to it by the blood. It changes some of them, breaking them down into smaller molecules. It stores others, especially glucose sugar, minerals such as iron, and vitamins such as B12. It also deals with possibly harmful substances, making them harmless; for example, it breaks down alcohol into less dangerous substances. This is called detoxification.

gall stones

Sometimes the gall bladder gets filled with hard lumps, on average about the size of a pea. These are gallstones. They are made from various substances, chiefly cholesterol and calcium. Cholesterol is a fatty substance that is essential for the body in small amounts. But too much can cause problems and clog up blood vessels. Gallstones can be seen on a cholecystogram X-ray photograph or scan (in green here). They can be removed by surgery or smashed into tiny pieces by very high-pitched sound waves (ultrasound).

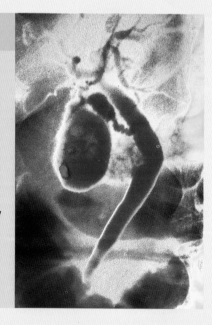

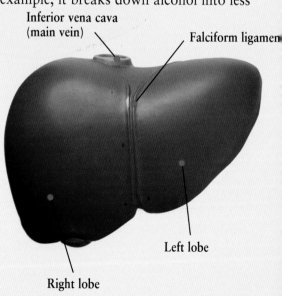

Inferior vena cava (main vein)

Falciform ligament

Left lobe

Right lobe

Normal front view of liver.

Caudate
lobe

Inferior vena cava
(main vein)

Hepatic artery and vein

Common bile duct

Right lobe

Cystic duct

Hepatic duct

Gall bladder

Quadrate lobe

Falciform ligament

View of the underside of the liver.

the liver lobule

This small clump of cells is about 1 mm (1.04 in) across, and there are many thousands in the entire liver. Each lobule contains hundreds of liver cells, known as hepatocytes. Like a living sponge, they are arranged in branching, curved sheets called cords or lamina, with spaces for blood, bile and other fluids between them. Between the lobules run miniature branches of the hepatic artery, the hepatic portal vein and the hepatic duct (for bile). Blood, rich in glucose, vitamins, minerals, nutrients and other liver-processed substances, is taken away along the larger branches of the main hepatic vein.

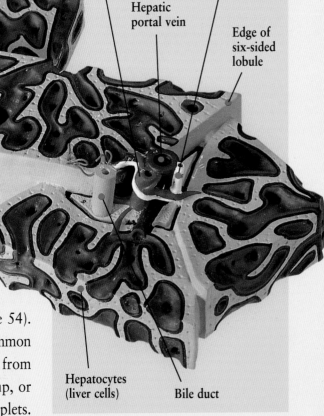

Hepatic artery

Lymphatic
vessel

Hepatic
portal vein

Edge of
six-sided
lobule

Hepatocytes
(liver cells)

Bile duct

The blood in the hepatic portal vein is low in oxygen, which it has already supplied to the walls of the stomach and intestines as well as to the spleen. Because of this the liver has its own separate blood supply from the hepatic artery, which is fresh with oxygen. All of the blood from the liver passes back to the heart, along the very wide but short, hepatic vein.

On the right underside of the liver is the gall bladder. It is a small bag that contains a yellowish fluid – bile. The liver makes up to 1 litre (1.76 pints) of bile every day. Some of this stays in the liver and some in the gall bladder – until you have a meal (see page 54). Then bile flows from the gall bladder and liver to a main tube, called the common bile duct, which empties it into the small intestine. Bile is a waste product from the liver, but it also helps with digestion. The mineral salts in it break up, or emulsify, fatty foods in the small intestine by turning the fats into tiny droplets.

I F YOU FEEL TOO HOT, you could do several things. You might remove some clothes and rest in a cool place, near a fan or in a breeze. You can splash water on your skin and have a cold drink. If you get too cold, you might move to a warmer place, put on more clothes and stay busy and active. These conscious actions help to keep the body at a fairly constant temperature of about 37 °C (98.4 °F). This happens despite the varying conditions on the outside. It also happens despite extra warmth from inside, because when your muscles are active they generate more heat, which tends to raise the body's temperature. If the temperature varies by more than a degree or two from 37 °C (98.4 °F), the body's chemistry is upset. The chemical processes and reactions do not happen properly. If temperature rises, you begin to feel ill and feverish. So body temperature is very important to keep constant.

A microscope view of a tiny sweat pore in the skin.

Your own internal thermostat

How does it work? The outside temperature is detected by sensitive nerve endings in the skin (see page 96). Your internal, or "core", body temperature is sensed in a small part of the brain called the hypothalamus. This is like the body's thermostat. If the internal temperature starts to rise, the hypothalamus switches on various processes which encourage the temperature to fall. Many of these are based in the skin. For example, the small blood vessels in your skin become wider, so that more blood flows near your body's

Erector   Narrowed   Hair follicle
pili muscle   blood vessel

This polar explorer's skin blood vessels are very narrow, so he looks pale. Each small skin hair (human "fur") is pulled upright by its tiny muscle, the erector pili, giving goose bumps. Wearing a hood is good, since the head can lose up to one-third of the body's heat.

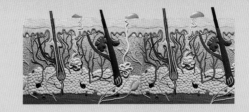

sweat gland

Each sweat gland is a knot of tubes and cells in the skin's lower layer, the dermis. A tube runs up to the skin's surface and opens at a hole called the sweat pore. You have about three million of these all over your body, although they are packed more closely in certain areas such as under your armpits, between your legs and on your forehead and temples.

surface and gives off its extra heat to the air. It also means that you look flushed. Three million or so tiny sweat glands in your skin release their watery sweat, or perspiration. It oozes onto the skin's surface and dries, or evaporates, drawing warmth from the body as it does so. The hypothalamus causes other parts of your brain to act consciously, making you change your clothes or move to another place. These actions also help to return your body temperature to normal.

Keeping warm

When the hypothalamus senses that core temperature is too low, it makes temperature-reducing processes go into reverse. The skin's small blood vessels get narrower, cutting heat loss and making you look pale. Sweating reduces to a minimum. The small hairs in your skin stand upright, with the aim of trapping air around the body as a heat-retaining layer. This produces goose bumps, or goose pimples, on the skin. (It's more obvious and works better in animals with longer hairs than ours. We say that they "fluff out their fur".) Your muscles might start to twitch and contract by themselves to generate some warmth. We call this shivering.

Sweat gland   Sweat droplet

After a good workout, the athlete looks sweaty and flushed. Blood collects heat from around her body and flows through the skin's widened vessels, passing the heat through the skin surface.

did you know?

► NORMAL BODY TEMPERATURE VARIES BETWEEN ABOUT 36.2 °C (97.1 °F) AND 37.3 °C (99.1 °F) DURING A NORMAL DAY.

► IN MOST PEOPLE IT IS LOWEST IN THE MIDDLE OF THE NIGHT OR EARLY IN THE MORNING, AROUND 3 OR 4 AM.

► AN ABNORMALLY HIGH BODY TEMPERATURE IS CALLED A FEVER, OR HYPERTHERMIA.

► A FEVER ABOVE 40 °C (104 °F) MAY CAUSE DRENCHING SWEAT, CONVULSIONS (FEBRILE FITS OR MUSCLE SPASMS) AND CONFUSION.

► AN ABNORMALLY LOW BODY TEMPERATURE IS CALLED HYPOTHERMIA.

► BODY TEMPERATURE BELOW 33 °C (91.4 °F) MAY CAUSE DROWSINESS AND CONFUSION.

the body's defences

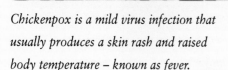

Chickenpox is a mild virus infection that usually produces a skin rash and raised body temperature – known as fever.

INVADERS ARE ALL AROUND. They are microscopic bacteria, viruses and other living things, too small to be seen without microscopes. They float in the air and land on our skin, clothes, food, drinks and other objects. If they get into the body, they could multiply and spread. Depending on the type of invader, they may cause one of the illnesses known as infections. These vary from a cold or sore throat which soon passes, to life-threatening pneumonia or tetanus. How does the body protect itself against invasion by these millions of microbes?

There are several types of surface defence to stop invaders getting into the body. Skin is a flexible barrier, very thick compared to the size of a germ. Normally, germs cannot get through it. You can help by washing away dirt and germs from your skin regularly. If there is a cut or other break in the skin, this is soon sealed by a blood clot, as described on later pages.

Delicate but defensive

Some parts of the body surface are not covered by skin, and they are very thin and delicate. Yet they are still well protected. The eyelids sweep dust, germs and other debris from the eyes every time you blink (see page 86). The insides of the nose, windpipe and lungs are covered with fluids that trap and remove germs. And germs in food or drink are killed by powerful acids and enzymes in the stomach.

But invaders sometimes get through the defences into blood and body parts. Then a complicated army of white blood cells goes into action. The white cells called macrophages and granulocytes engulf and eat germs whole. Some of the white cells, known as lymphocytes, make body proteins called antibodies. These stick onto the germs and kill or disable them. As the battle rages, white cells travel and multiply in the blood and lymph fluid. They also gather in various lymph tissues – lymph nodes (see page 60), the thymus gland in the neck, the spleen to the left of the stomach, the adenoids at the back of the nose, the tonsils at the back of the throat, and parts of the intestines. These lymph tissues may enlarge or swell as dead germs, white blood cells and fluids collect inside them. This is the reason why an infection produces

immunization

The body can be "tricked" into fighting a type of invader by injecting it with a dead or harmless version of it. This is what happens when you have a vaccination, or inoculation. The immune defence system goes through the process of destroying the germ and is then ready to recognize it again in the future. This is called immunization. Large-scale immunization of millions of people against infections such as polio, tetanus, measles, rubella and mumps, is one of modern medicine's greatest successes.

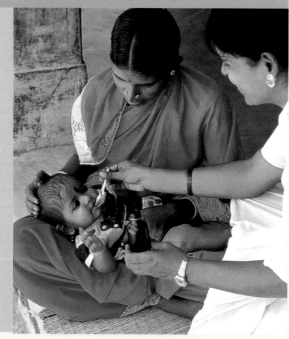

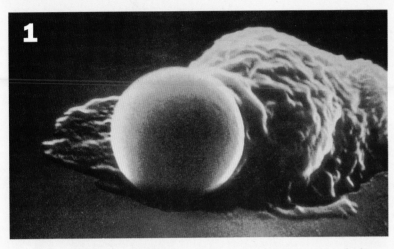

The scanning electron microscope reveals a macrophage, a type of white blood cell, oozing and approaching its "victim".

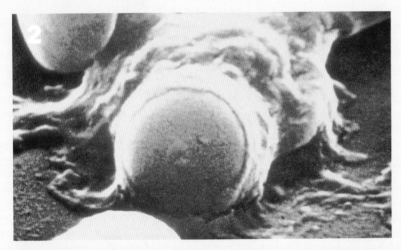

The victim is a red blood cell, which has reached the end of its life and become ball-shaped. It is ready for recycling.

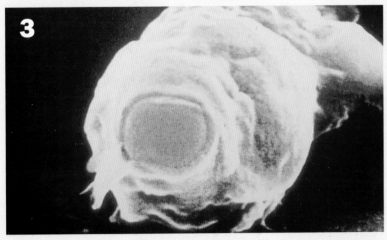

The macrophage spreads around, engulfs and digests the old red cell, by the process known as cellular phagocytosis.

"swollen glands". The battle involves lots of chemical activity, so body temperature rises and produces a fever. But usually the germs are gradually defeated.

Prepared for future fights

Lymphocytes also prepare for the future. Once they encounter a type of germ, they are ready to recognize it quickly if it invades again. Then they kill it off before it can multiply and cause illness. This means that once we have had certain infections we are protected from, or immune to, them. The system that produces this protection, involving white cells and lymph and other parts, is the body's immune defence system.

Invaders enter the body in various ways, called routes of infection. They are breathed in as tiny droplets in the air, especially after someone sneezes. They are taken in with food and drink, as in some types of food poisoning. They spread by physical touch and on objects such as towels. They are also spread by carriers or vectors, including animal pests such as lice, fleas, flies and mosquitoes.

the stages of infection

If germs get into the body and begin to multiply, this starts an infection. The episode usually goes through several stages. During the incubation period, the germs have gained a foothold in the body. They are present and building up their numbers, but they cause few outward signs or symptoms. During this time the person may be infectious, able to spread the germs to others by various means, and even contagious, that is able to spread the germs by direct physical contact. The incubation period varies greatly, from a few days in colds and influenza, to many years with HIV, the virus germ that causes AIDS. Next is the symptomatic period, when the person suffers symptoms associated with the disease. These vary according to the germ concerned, but they usually include fever, soreness, aches and pains. There usually follows the recovery period as the body's defences get the upper hand and the germs are gradually killed.

cuts and breaks

THE BODY HAS AMAZING ABILITIES to keep itself in good working order by carrying out "running repairs". Any small damage caused by being knocked, squashed or twisted is soon put right by the maintenance and mending systems. The most familiar is when blood in a wound forms a sticky lump called a clot. The clot fills the gap, seals the wound edges and stops leakage out, keeps germs and other unwanted items getting in, and then starts healing. This happens not only in cuts and wounds to the skin that we can see. It's also going on every day at a microscopic level throughout the inside of the body, when tiny leaks in various vessels are sealed.

Clot to scab to scar

As soon as cells are damaged in a cut or wound, they release chemicals that trigger a remarkable series of events. A substance called fibrinogen is normally invisible and dissolved in the blood. But when damage happens, fibrinogen combines with chemicals released by the cell fragments in the blood, called platelets. These turn the fibrinogen into fibrin, which is a net or mesh of minute fibres. Red cells, white cells and more platelets get stuck among the fibres. The platelets go sticky and only a few minutes after the damage occurs, a clot begins to form and plug the wound.

More white blood cells arrive at the scene and begin to eat any germs and other debris. The fibres in the clot contract and make it shrink, drawing the edges together and hardening it into a scab. Meanwhile, yet more cells, including fibroblasts, gather at the spot. They make fibres of collagen to strengthen the area – a scar. By now the normal cells that make up the area are multiplying, to spread and mend the damage.

giving blood

Hospitals and medical centres need daily supplies of blood for accident victims, emergencies and operations. Blood can be kept in cold store, either whole or separated into parts like red cells and plasma. But eventually it goes stale and useless. So blood donations are very important and new donors are always welcomed.

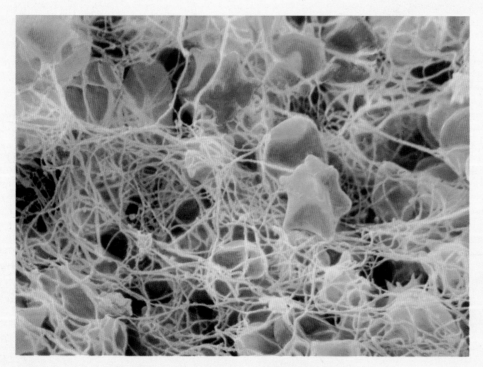

Sticky strands of fibrin enmesh blood cells and begin to form a clot.

Blood transfusions

Sometimes a cut is too big to seal in this way. The body can be helped by medical techniques like sutures (stitches) or clips which hold the wound closed. However, if blood loss is too great, the doctors may consider performing a blood transfusion. This means putting blood from one person,

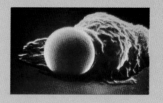

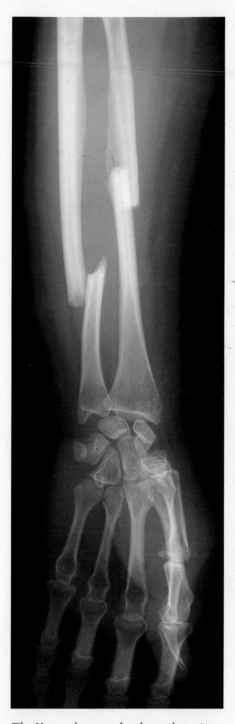

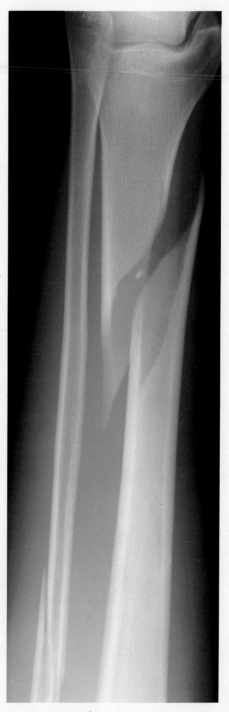

The X-ray photographs above show, in the left picture, broken ulna and radius bones (ouch!), located in the forearm, and in the right picture, a broken tibia bone in the shin.

invisible mending

A broken or fractured bone can mend itself if the stresses and strains are taken off it for a time. This can be done by putting splints or a cast on the outside or by fixing metal or plastic supports inside the body with screws and glues. First, the blood vessels grow and new cartilage forms across the break. This is turned into bone, and finally any lumps are smoothed away to leave a virtually invisible mend. The smoothing-off process is called remodelling. Like many of the body's repair and mending systems, bone healing becomes less efficient with age. This means that an older person's bones are usually weaker and more brittle, and they take a longer time to heal when they are broken.

the donor, into another person, the recipient. But different people have blood of different types called blood groups – the A, B, O and Rhesus systems are the main ones.

If blood from a certain group is put into a recipient of another group, it may form lumps and clots, and endanger life. So the blood groups of donor and recipient must be carefully tested and "matched". During surgery, blood is likely to leak from incisions. Again, it can be replaced by blood transfusions. During a complex operation the team may use more than 50 litres (12.5 gallons) of blood to keep the patient alive and safe. Many blood products are purified from whole blood, for treating certain disorders. Purified factor VII treats the "bleeding disease" called haemophilia, in which blood fails to clot properly.

chapter

5

the senses

THE HUMAN BODY is very sensitive. It can detect many different aspects of its surroundings – light rays, sound waves, chemicals floating through the air, and temperature without even touching. This gives it information

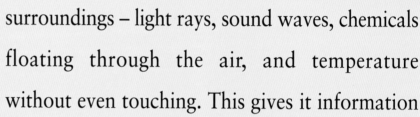

about distant events. At closer quarters, the body can detect physical contact and whether an object is hot or cold, hard or soft,

smooth or rough, and still or moving. The body can also make out certain chemicals in foods and drinks.

These powers of detection come from our five main senses of sight, hearing, smell, touch and taste. But the body has

other senses, too. It can assess the positions of its limbs and other parts as they move about. It can detect gravity and motion. Internal sensors monitor the levels of chemicals, such as blood sugar.

So the senses tell the body about the world outside, and also about its world within. Acting on this information, the body can then take action to cope and ensure its own survival.

a sight for your eyes

THE EYES ARE THE BODY'S WINDOWS on the world. Like a video camera, they detect a full-colour moving picture of the world and turn it into tiny electrical signals. Of course, unlike a video camera, these signals are not stored on a magnetic tape. The signals are nerve impulses, which go to the brain for sorting. In ancient times, people thought that light shone out of their eyes onto what they looked at. Now we know that light rays pass from an object into the eye. When you look at an object, the light from it enters your eye through a very thin, transparent "skin" – the conjunctiva. This senses anything that touches it, like dust. Every second or two, the eyelids blink and sweep tear fluid across the conjunctiva, washing away dust and germs.

Behind the conjunctiva is the transparent domed front of the eye – the cornea. It bends, or focuses, the light rays so that they will give a clear picture by the time they get to the back of the eye. Next, the rays pass through a hole called the pupil, in a circular coloured sheet of muscle – the iris.

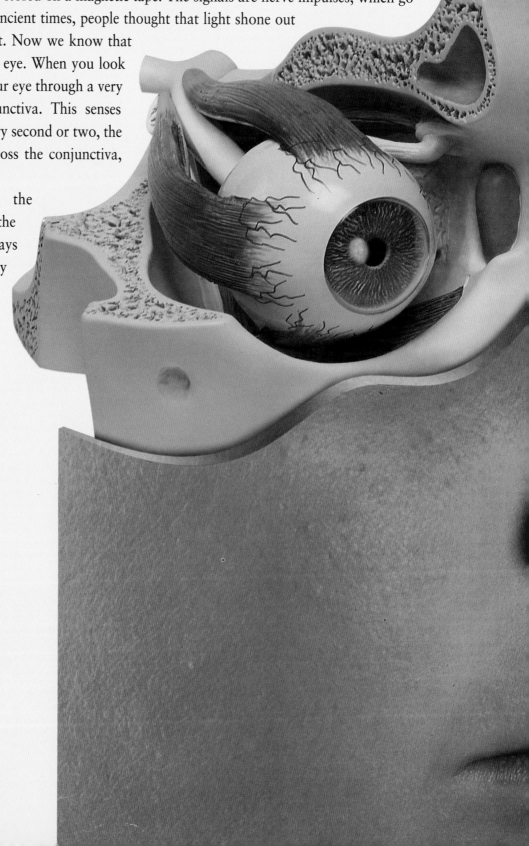

the eyeball

An eyeball is about 25 mm (1 in) across. It nestles well protected in a bowl-shaped socket called the orbit, formed by the skull bones. The tough, outer white coat of the eyeball is the sclera. You can see it at the front as the "white of the eye" around the coloured iris and the dark hole of the pupil. Between the eyeball and the orbit are six small muscles, fixed to the sclera near the front and to the bones of the socket at the rear. They contract or relax as a team to move the eye around as you look up, down and to either side.

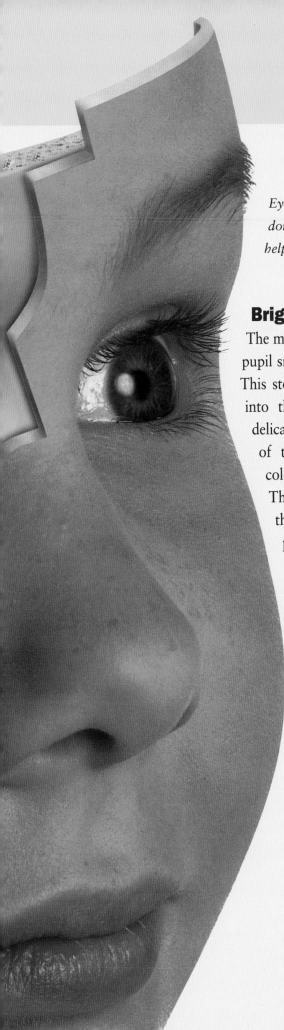

Eyebrows stop water dripping down into the eyes. Eyelashes help to keep out dust.

Bright eyes

The muscles contract to make the pupil smaller in bright conditions. This stops too much light getting into the eye and damaging its delicate inner parts. The colour of the iris gives the eye its colour, such as blue or brown. The light rays carry on through another transparent part – the lens. It is shaped like the lens in a camera and does a similar job. It adds to the focusing power of the cornea and makes fine adjustments, depending on whether the object is near or far away. In a camera, the lens focuses by moving backwards and forwards. The eye's lens is slightly elastic and focuses by changing shape. After the lens, the light rays go through the clear jelly in the middle of the eyeball, to the retina, which is shown on the next page.

focusing

A ring of muscles around the lens – the ciliary muscles – changes its shape. The muscles contract to make the lens become thicker and more bulging. This bends rays from nearby objects more, to make sure that they cast a sharp, clear view or image onto the back of the eye. The ciliary muscles relax when looking at faraway objects, and the lens becomes thinner, to bend the rays less.

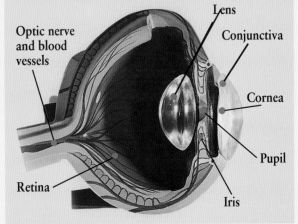

Optic nerve and blood vessels

Lens

Conjunctiva

Cornea

Pupil

Iris

Retina

the eye in its socket

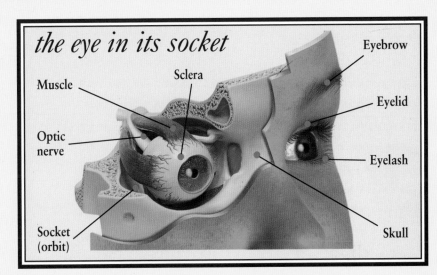

Muscle

Sclera

Optic nerve

Socket (orbit)

Eyebrow

Eyelid

Eyelash

Skull

from eye to brain

Taller rod cells (lilac) outnumber cone cells (blue) in the retina.

WHEN LIGHT RAYS HAVE PASSED through the cornea and lens, they shine onto the rear inner surface of the eyeball, a layer called the retina. It is not much bigger than a postage stamp, and even thinner. Yet it contains more than 130 million microscopic cells. When light shines on them, they generate nerve signals – that is, they are light sensitive.

There are two types of light-sensitive cell in the retina, named after their shapes – rods and cones. Rods are far more numerous, at about 125 million. They respond to all types of light, whether white, red, blue, green, yellow or any other colour. So they cannot tell the difference between colours. But rods do work with very weak light, so they help the eye to see well in dim conditions. As you peer through the gathering gloom of the evening, and everything seems grey as colours fade, you are using mainly the rods in your eyes.

The other type of light-sensitive cell is the cone. There are about 7 million of them in the retina, clustered mainly around the back, opposite the lens. Cones do not respond to weak light rays, so they cannot see in dim conditions. But they can see colours.

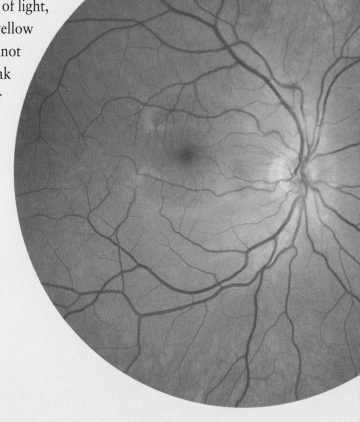

the image

The picture, or image, that shines on the retina has been focused by the cornea and lens so that it is clear and sharp. But like any image formed by a lens, it is upside down and back to front. However, the brain learns and becomes programmed from birth, to link an image at a certain place on the retina with an object in a certain position in the real world, out in front of the person. We never know any different, so the upside-down and back-to-front image never causes problems.

the blind spot

All the nerve fibres from different parts of the retina come together at the optic disc, and pass out of the eye into the optic nerve. There are no light-sensitive cells at the optic disc, so it cannot see anything. It is also known as the blind spot. Normally the eye moves about quickly, and the brain gets used to filling in the gap of the blind spot, so we never notice it. Also, the blind spots of both eyes hardly ever coincide, so information from one eye is used to fill the gap from the other eye's blind spot.

judging distance

The two eyes point at the view from slightly different angles, so they see slightly different images. The brain compares these images: they differ more the nearer to the object they are. The brain also receives feedback from the eye muscles about where each eye is looking. Again, the more the eyes point inward, the nearer the object they are. This information from two eyes allows us to judge distance and depth to give a three-dimensional view. It is called stereoscopic or binocular vision.

Sight tests check for disease as well as good vision.

short and long sight

With short sight, faraway objects look blurred. This is usually due to the eyeball being too large for the focusing power of the cornea and lens. With long sight, near objects look blurred because the eyeball is too small for the focusing power of the cornea and lens. These problems of vision can be helped by adding extra lenses, either in spectacles or as a contact lens on the cornea. A recent advance is to "sculpture" the cornea by burning off bits with a fine laser beam to adjust its focusing power.

the retina

Cones are packed together mainly at the rear of the eye, opposite the lens. When you look at something to study it in detail, its image falls onto this area, which is known as the yellow spot, or fovea. Under the retina is the choroid, a layer rich in blood vessels. It nourishes the retina on its inside and the sclera on its outside.

There are three types of cone, and each type responds best to either red, yellow-green or blue light. Working together, they can pick up light in mixtures of hues and see tiny details.

The rods and cones pass their nerve signals to nerve cells in the retina. The signals then go along more nerve cells to the optic nerve, which carries them from the back of the eye to the brain. In the visual centres at the rear of the brain (see page 102), the signals are sorted, analysed and compared to produce your "mind's eye" view of the world.

Eyeing up the problem

Eyes are delicate and sensitive, and sometimes affected by disease. Conjunctivitis is swelling, itching and soreness of the conjunctiva, the very thin surface layer over the cornea. In a sight test, an optician usually examines the inside of the eye, especially looking at the lens and retina. The inside of the eye is one of the few places in the body where living blood vessels can be seen clearly. Their condition gives information about health problems such as high blood pressure or diabetes.

colour blindness

In each eye, you have cone cells sensitive to either red, yellowish-green or blue light. About 1 in 12 boys and 1 in 200 girls are unable to distinguish certain colours because some of their cone cells do not function properly. In test one (left), only people with normal vision will see a loop of pink and orange dots. In test two (right), normal people will see the number 5 while those with defective red-green vision will see a number 2.

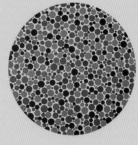 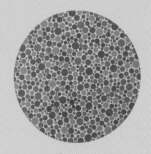

Test one *Test two*

sound sense

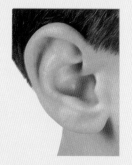

HEARING INVOLVES MUCH MORE than the ears on the side of your head. These are the outer ears or ear flaps, made of skin-covered cartilage. In our evolutionary past, our distant ancestors may have had bigger and more trumpet-shaped ears, which they could move and swivel to pick up and pinpoint sounds. In today's human body, the only leftover sign of this is that some people can wiggle their ears slightly.

Good vibrations

Sounds pass through the air as vibrations – invisible ripples of high and low air pressure called sound waves. The outer ear helps to catch sound waves and direct them into the hole in its middle. This is the ear canal, which is about half as long as your little finger. The canal ends at a thin, flexible, sheet – like skin – called the eardrum. It is roughly the area of your little fingernail.

The vibrations of sound waves bounce off the eardrum and make it vibrate too. On the inner side of the drum is an air-filled chamber called the middle ear. It contains a set of three tiny bones, each smaller than a baked bean. They are the hammer, anvil and stirrup. They are joined by miniature joints and have tiny muscles to move them, just like the larger bones of the main skeleton. The hammer is fixed to the inner side of the eardrum. So as the drum vibrates and shakes and rattles, the vibrations pass to the hammer, which sends them to the anvil and then to the stirrup. The base of the stirrup lies against a snail-shaped part called the cochlea, deep inside the skull. So the vibrations then pass into the cochlea. The rest of the story is on the next page.

A doctor looks into the ear using an auriscope (otoscope), with a light and lens.

the three-part ear

The outer ear collects sound waves, which are vibrations in air. The middle ear turns them into vibrations in solids – the ear drum and tiny bones. The inner ear changes them into vibrations in fluid, and then into electrical nerve signals. The middle and inner ears are protected from knocks by skull bones. The hairs and waxy lining of the outer ear canal gather and remove dust and germs.

Frequency and decibels

Sounds are all around us. Even on the quietest day there is the whisper of wind, the rustle of grass or leaves, the hum of distant traffic and the rumble of a faraway aeroplane. Some sounds are deep, or low in pitch, or frequency, like a thunderclap or a bass guitar. Others are shrill, high in pitch or frequency, such as twittering birds or the "ssss" of a cymbal. Our ears can detect many pitches or frequencies of sounds, but not all of them. Frequency is measured in units called Hertz, (Hz). Human ears respond to sounds from about 25 up to 20,000 Hz. Our ability to hear high-pitched sounds decreases with

The ear drum is a thin sheet of skin-like substance.

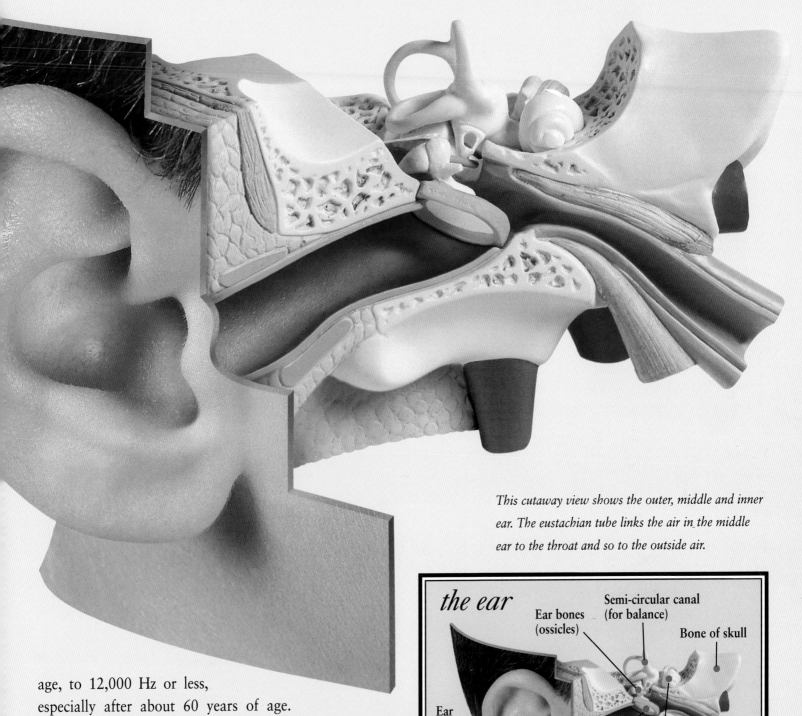

This cutaway view shows the outer, middle and inner ear. The eustachian tube links the air in the middle ear to the throat and so to the outside air.

age, to 12,000 Hz or less, especially after about 60 years of age. Many animals, such as dogs, bats and dolphins, can hear far higher-pitched sounds.

The other main feature of sound is its loudness or volume. This is measured in decibels, (dB). We can just about detect a sound of 10 dB, like a ticking watch. Very loud noises over about 90 dB, like jet engines, road drills and too-powerful loudspeakers, can damage our ears.

the ear

Ear bones (ossicles)

Semi-circular canal (for balance)

Bone of skull

Ear flap (pinna)

Outer ear canal

Eardrum (tympanic membrane)

Cochlea in inner ear

Eustachian tube

hearing

Balance relies on many sense organs, including the ears, eyes, skin and muscle sensors.

LIKE THE BODY'S OTHER SENSES, hearing involves the process called transduction. This means that energy in one form, in this case sound waves, is changed to energy in another form – tiny electrical nerve signals. All the sense organs, including the eyes, nose, tongue and skin, carry out transduction. This means changing the energy of the feature they sense into electrical nerve signals.

The part of the ear that transduces is the cochlea. It is in the inner ear, deep inside the skull, just behind and below the eye. It is a fluid-filled tube coiled in a tall spiral like a snail's shell. Inside the cochlea is a jelly-like sheet or membrane. Just below this are rows of specially sensitive hair cells on another sheet – the basement membrane. These cells have micro-hairs sticking out of them. The tips of the hairs are embedded in the jelly-like sheet above.

The vibrations made by sound waves pass from the stirrup bone into the cochlea fluid. They set up ripples that shake the membranes. The shaking pulls on the micro-hairs, which makes the hair cells generate nerve signals. These flash along the cochlear nerve to the brain. Different pitches and volumes of sound set the cochlear membranes vibrating in different way, creating different patterns of nerve signals. In the brain, the signals are sorted and compared, to give you your sense of hearing.

supersenses

Humans have fairly sharp all-round senses. But some animals have much better sensory equipment. One piece of sensory equipment is often very well developed, usually because they need it to hunt their prey. An owl can hear five times better than us. And a hawk or eagle can see details of an object at eight times the distance we can.

Use your ears to balance yourself

The ear also helps with balance. Near the cochlea are more fluid-filled tubes – the semicircular canals. As your head moves about, the fluid inside each canal swishes to and fro. This pushes and pulls on a blob of jelly containing minerals which sticks out into the fluid in a larger part of the canal known as the ampulla. Micro-hairs of sensitive hair cells are embedded in the mineral blob. As the blob moves, the hair cells generate nerve signals and send them along the vestibular nerve to the brain. The brain can tell which way the head is moving. Similar hair cells in other parts of the ear, the saccule and utricle, have their micro-hairs embedded in

balance and the ear

"Balance" is not a single sense. It is a continuing process involving input from senses such as the motion and gravity detectors in the inner ear, the eyes, skin, muscles and joints; and output of instructions to the muscles for balancing postures and movements.

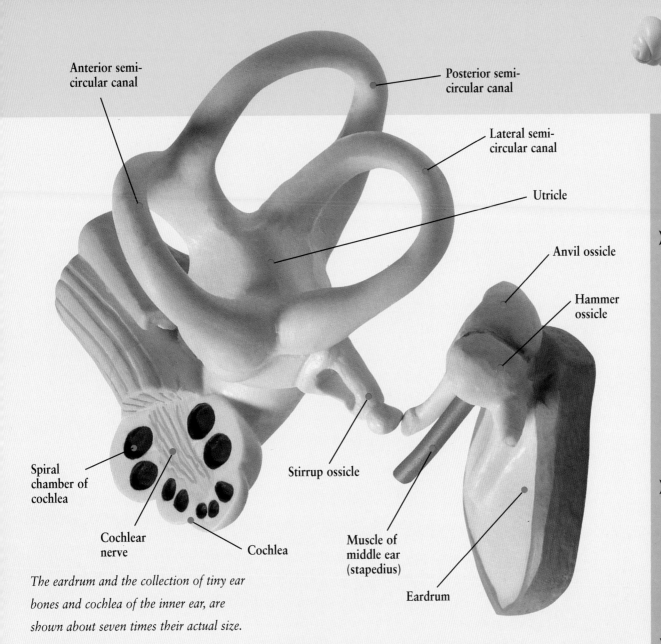

Anterior semi-
circular canal

Posterior semi-
circular canal

Lateral semi-
circular canal

Utricle

Anvil ossicle

Hammer
ossicle

Spiral
chamber of
cochlea

Cochlear
nerve

Cochlea

Stirrup ossicle

Muscle of
middle ear
(stapedius)

Eardrum

*The eardrum and the collection of tiny ear
bones and cochlea of the inner ear, are
shown about seven times their actual size.*

mineral lumps that are pulled down
by gravity. As you move your head,
the pull of gravity changes and so
you sense which way is up and
which is down.

inside the cochlea

The sets of membranes and hair cells
that vibrate inside the cochlea are called
the organ of Corti, after the Italian
microscope expert Alfonso Corti. He
described them in 1851. There are about
15,000 hair cells (shown here), and some
of them have more than 100 micro-hairs.

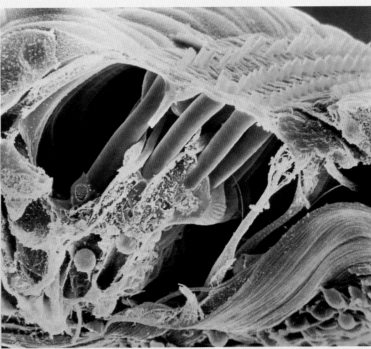

did you know?

▶ THE THREE
SEMICIRCULAR CANALS
ARE SET AT RIGHT ANGLES
TO EACH OTHER:
UP–DOWN, FRONT–BACK
AND SIDE–SIDE.
WHICHEVER WAY THE HEAD
MOVES, IT DISTURBS
FLUID IN ONE OF THE
CANALS.

▶ THE UTRICLE AND
SACCULE ARE ALSO AT
RIGHT ANGLES TO EACH
OTHER, SO THEY DETECT
GRAVITY AND DIRECTION
OF HEAD MOVEMENTS.

▶ BALANCE INVOLVES
OTHER SENSES, TOO. THE
EYES NOTE HORIZONTAL
THINGS LIKE FLOORS AND
WATER SURFACES, AND
VERTICAL LINES LIKE
WALLS AND TREES.

▶ THE SKIN DETECTS
PRESSURE ON VARIOUS
PARTS, ESPECIALLY THE
SOLES OF THE FEET, TO
GET INFORMATION ABOUT
THE DOWNWARD PULL OF
GRAVITY.

93

smell and taste

WHEN YOU HAVE A COLD and a stuffed-up nose, you cannot smell very well. Oddly, you don't taste properly either. Food seems bland and flavourless. This is not because a cold affects your sense of taste. Smell in the nose, and taste on the tongue, are two separate senses that work independently. However, when you taste the flavours of food, you also smell its odours. They waft from your mouth up through its rear roof, into your nose. So taste and smell often occur together, and your brain associates them with one another.

There is another link between taste and smell. They both detect molecules or chemicals, so are called chemosenses. Smell works by recognizing odour molecules floating in the air. Taste senses flavour molecules in foods and drinks which get dissolved in the saliva inside the mouth as you chew.

hairy smellers

The cells that "smell" are tall and thin, and crammed together with supporting cells. Their spaghetti-like hairs are up to 0.2 mm (0.008 in) long. They stick into the layer of thin, watery mucus which coats the whole of the inside of the nose. It's thought that odour molecules of different shapes dissolve in the mucus and try to fit into similar-shaped holes, or receptor sites, on the hairs. When one slots in, like a key in a lock, this produces a nerve signal.

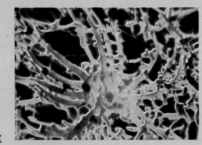

How you smell

As you breathe in, odour molecules float into your nose and through the nasal cavity behind it. If you wish to smell something carefully, you sniff at it. The sniff makes air swirl around in the top of the nasal cavity and brings the odour molecules into contact with two patches of hairy cells there – the olfactory epithelia. When certain odour molecules land on the cells' hairs, the cells generate nerve signals. These signals pass up to a clump of nerves just above – the olfactory bulb – where they are partly sorted. Then they continue along the olfactory nerve to the olfactory, or smell, centre in the brain.

Tastes are detected by thousands of taste buds, scattered along the tip, sides and back of the tongue. There are also some near the lips, on the roof and sides of the mouth, and in the upper throat. Each taste bud is tiny – it's a microscopic bunch of about 50 cells which have furry, frilly tips. There are four main types of taste: sweet, sour, salty and bitter. When flavour molecules land on the frilly tip, the tastebud cells make nerve signals. These pass along small nerves which gather into two main nerves – the seventh and ninth cranial nerves (see page 100). The signals travel along these to the gustatory, or taste, centres in the brain.

frilly tasters

The cells that "taste" are grouped into a ball – the taste bud. Finger-shaped microvilli give their tips a furry appearance. Flavour molecules in food seep through the saliva in the mouth, and through a small opening in the tongue's surface, to reach the microvilli of the taste bud. The molecules may fit into specially shaped receptors in lock-and-key fashion, like smell.

94

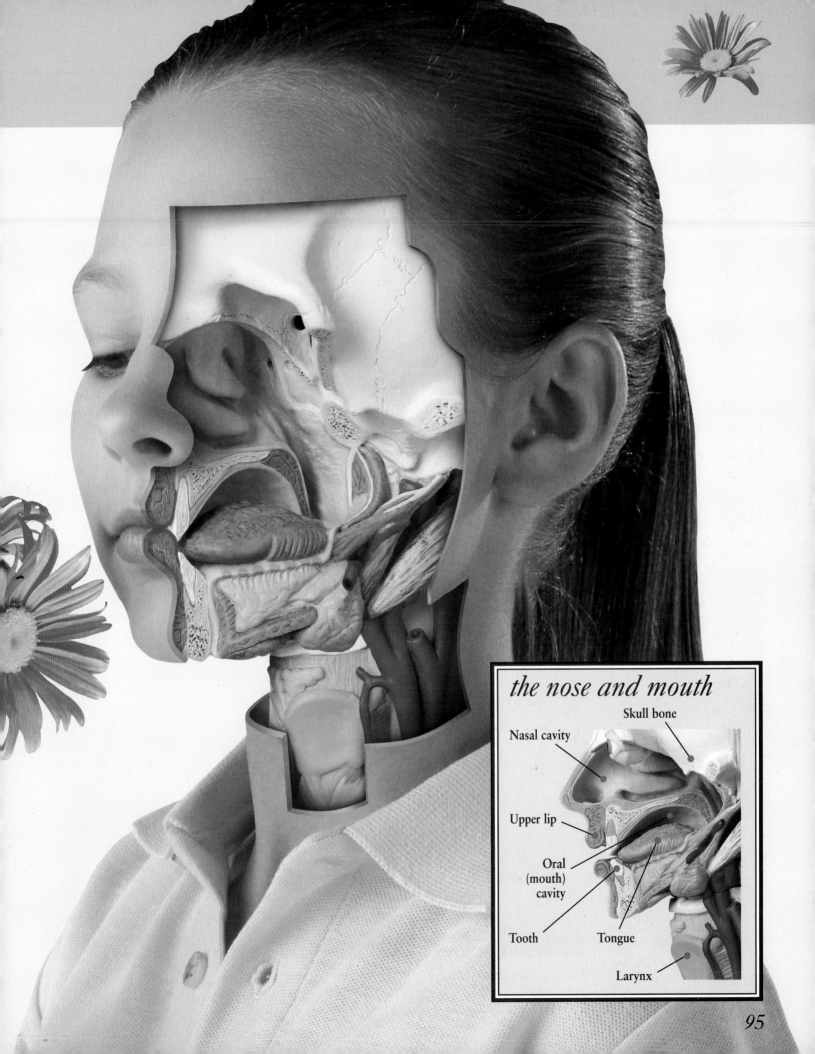

the nose and mouth

Skull bone

Nasal cavity

Upper lip

Oral
(mouth)
cavity

Tooth

Tongue

Larynx

the multi-touch sense

The ridges on a fingertip help with grip and the sense of touch.

CLOSE YOUR EYES AND TOUCH something, such as your clothes, a table, a car or your own skin. Stroke it gently. What does it feel like? Is it hard or soft, hot or cold? The surface may be smooth, bumpy, gritty, furry or hairy. It could be dry, moist or slimy. Some objects, such as a fridge or car, might be moving or vibrating slightly due to a motor. If the object has sharp edges or points and you press too hard, you might even feel slight pain. A pet such as a cat or dog feels warm and "alive". This simple test shows that the skin's sense of touch is really a multi-sense. It can feel many different features. It does this using dozens of microscopic sensors packed into every square millimetre of skin. There are several different kinds and shapes of sensor. When they are squashed, squeezed, pressed, heated, cooled, stretched or altered one way or another, they make nerve signals that go to the brain.

How do you feel and what can you feel?

skin sensors

The touch micro-sensors in skin are found at different depths in its layers. Most of them are named after the Italian or German microscope experts who studied them in detail – Pacini, Ruffini, Krause and Meissner. By far the largest are the Pacinian sensors, which may be up to 0.5 mm (2/100 in) long, just about visible to the naked eye. Free nerve endings are like tiny bushes of naked nerves. They sense pain.

It was once thought that each kind of sensor detected one feature, such as heat or heavy pressure. But it seems that the real picture is more complicated. It's based on pattern recognition. Working together, the sensors send complex patterns of nerve signals to the brain. The brain assesses the patterns. It's like

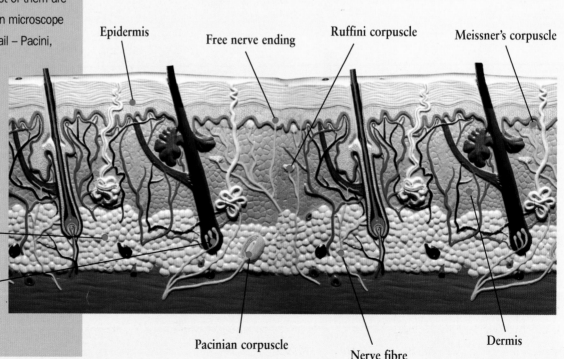

Epidermis

Free nerve ending

Ruffini corpuscle

Meissner's corpuscle

Hypodermis

Hair-root sensor

Pacinian corpuscle

Nerve fibre

Dermis

studying a mosaic – the pieces do not mean much on their own. But put them together and you recognize the overall pattern – in this case, the whole touch picture.

Pattern recognition is important in the way that the brain sorts nerve signals from all the senses. And, with all the senses, the brain interprets the pattern of nerve signals according to information built up in its memory over the years. So you can recognize the shape and feel of a plastic beaker or a pile of baked beans by your "touch memory", without seeing them.

nails

Fingernails and toenails are like sheets of dead, hardened, compressed skin. They are made mainly of the body protein keratin (see page 97), the same substance that forms the claws and hooves of other mammals. The nail grows from its root, under the skin along its attached edge – the cuticle. On average, fingernails grow about 1 mm (0.04 in) in one week. If you do heavy work with you hands, your fingernails may be worn away almost as fast. Toenails grow slightly more slowly than fingernails.

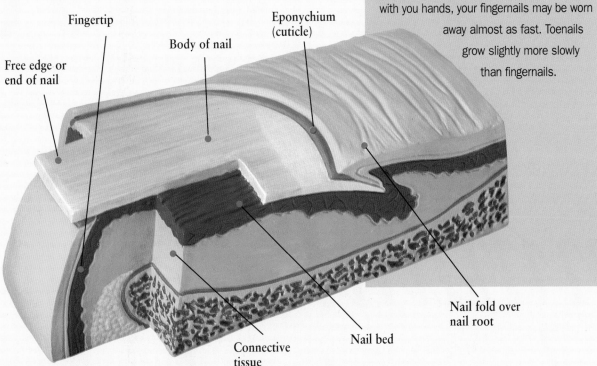

Fingertip

Body of nail

Eponychium (cuticle)

Free edge or end of nail

Connective tissue

Nail bed

Nail fold over nail root

How sensitive are you?

The skin's micro-sensors are not scattered evenly over the body. Some areas have thousands of sensors packed into a small area, as on the lips and fingertips. The fingers are good at feeling light touch and vibrations. The skin on the elbow is not very sensitive to light touch but it can feel temperatures well. This is why a baby's bathwater is often tested by dipping your elbow into it, rather than your hand. Some patches of skin, such as the upper arms and the thighs, have very few touch micro-sensors and so are not very sensitive.

Hairs and nails are made of dead material, so they cannot feel anything. However, hairs have micro-sensors wrapped around their roots. As the hair rocks, it moves the micro-sensors and makes them produce nerve signals. Similarly, the skin around and under a fingernail or toenail has micro-sensors, which respond when the nail is pressed or moved.

did you know?

➤ NAILS GROW SLIGHTLY FASTER IN SUMMER THAN IN WINTER, ESPECIALLY FINGERNAILS.

➤ FINGERNAILS ALSO GROW SLIGHTLY FASTER ON THE FAVOURED HAND – FOR EXAMPLE, THE RIGHT HAND OF A RIGHT-HANDED PERSON – THAN ON THE OTHER HAND.

➤ THESE DIFFERENCES ARE PROBABLY DUE TO THE SLIGHTLY HIGHER TEMPERATURE OF THE FAVOURED HAND (SINCE ITS MUSCLES ARE MORE ACTIVE AND GENERATE MORE HEAT), AND THE EXTRA WARMTH IN SUMMER COMPARED TO WINTER.

➤ NAILS HAVE SEVERAL USES: THEY PROTECT THE FINGER AND TOE ENDS, THEY FORM A STIFF PAD OR SHEET AGAINST WHICH THE SKIN SENSES PRESSURE, AND THEY RELIEVE ITCHES – BY SCRATCHING!

chapter

6

HAVE YOU EVER been alone in a quiet place, staying still and silent? For a time, it might be restful and relaxing; but after a while you could get bored. You may want to do something, like twiddle your thumbs or talk to someone. Humans are

communication and control

basically social creatures, and usually we enjoy the company of others. We like to communicate. Inside the human body, communication is also vital. All the

parts and organs must communicate with one another and be controlled, so that they work together in a coordinated way for the good of the whole being. The body system specialized for communication, control and coordination is the nervous system. Its main part is the control centre of the entire body, and the place where you think, behave, have ideas and remember – the brain. This is connected to almost every body part by the neural network of nerves.

a bundle of nerves

A TELECOMMUNICATIONS SYSTEM links phones, faxes, computers and other machines by bundles of electrical wires or fibre-optic cables. The body has communication bundles, too. They are the nerves. They carry messages as tiny electrical pulses called nerve signals. These are the "language" of the body's control and communication system. The main and thickest nerve is the spinal cord, inside the backbone. Smaller nerves branch from it into all the different parts of your body. The longest nerves snake between organs, right down to your fingertips and toes. They look like lengths of smooth, shiny, greyish string. Joined to the top of the spinal cord, and almost filling the upper half of the head, is the brain. It is grey-pink and has the consistency of jelly or blancmange. The brain is well protected from being knocked and squashed by the rigid dome of the skull bones.

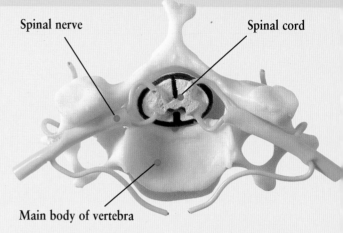

Spinal nerve   Spinal cord

Main body of vertebra

The spinal cord is encased inside the individual bones of the backbone, called the vertebrae.

You are a live wire

Like other body parts, the brain and nerves are made from cells. They are nerve cells, or neurones. They have a very long, thin part called an axon, which is like a "living wire" to carry nerve signals. The axons of some nerve cells are over 30 cm (1 ft) long, although they are incredibly thin, like super-fine hairs, visible only under a microscope. The main part of a nerve cell, called the cell body, is much the same size as in other cells, around 0.01–0.05 mm (0.0004–0.002 in) across. The cell body has smaller spidery projections, called dendrites. The branched ends of the axon from one nerve cell nearly touch the dendrites of other nerve cells. Tiny gaps – synapses – separate them. Nerve signals can jump the gap and pass from one nerve cell to another. The brain has at least 100 million nerve cells, arranged in layers, cables and bundles. Each nerve cell may have so many dendrites that is in touch with over 100,000 other nerve cells, sending and receiving signals from them. The enormous complexity of the neural network of the brain is mind-boggling.

the spinal column

The spinal cord is contained inside a tunnel formed by the lined-up holes through the row of vertebral bones which make up the spine (vertebral column). The bones protect it and prevent it from getting kinked or twisted (except in back injuries). The spinal cord runs from the base of the skull down to the first lower-back or lumbar vertebra. Here it splits into smaller, separate nerves.

You've got a nerve

The spinal cord and nerves are made mainly from bundles of long, thin axons lying side by side. In a nerve the thickness of a piece of cotton, such as the one that goes to the eyeball-moving muscles, there may be a few hundred axons. In a nerve as thick as your thumb, like the sciatic nerve in the hip, there are millions of axons. Some nerve cells transmit signals to the brain from a sense organ such as the skin, eye or tongue. These cells are sensory neurones. Other nerve cells with their axons carry signals from the brain out to the muscles, telling them when to contract. These are motor neurones. Many of the body's major nerves contain both sensory and motor neurones.

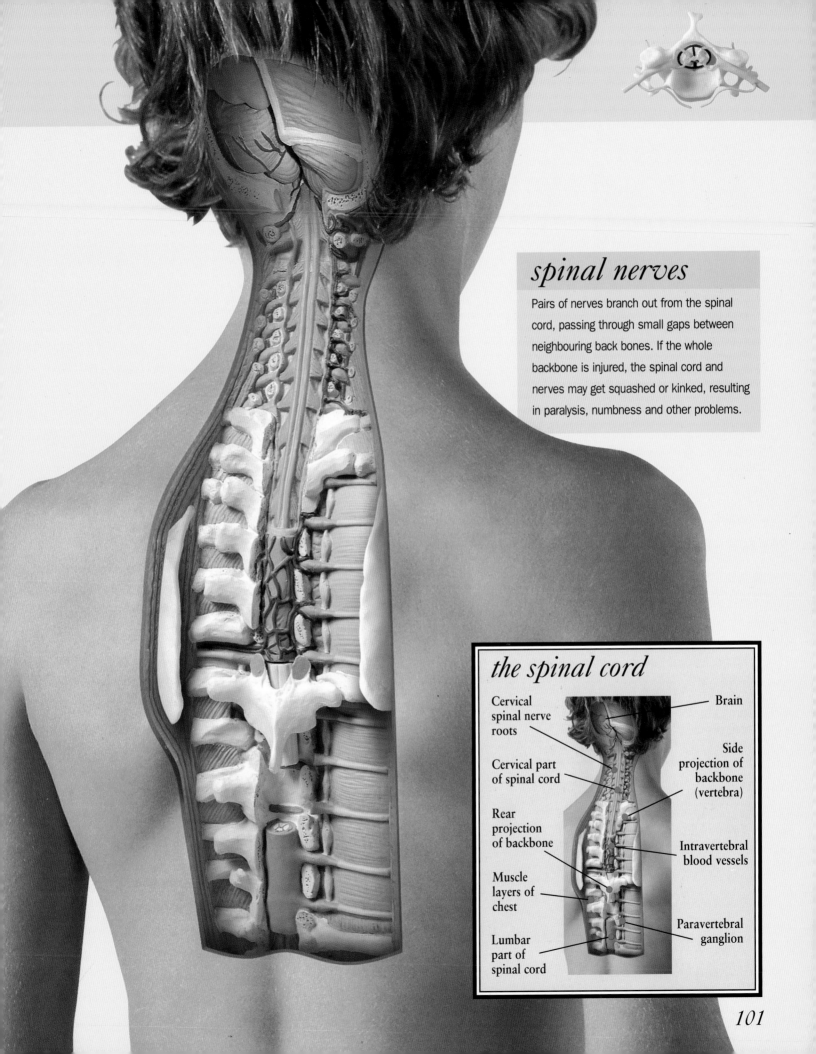

spinal nerves

Pairs of nerves branch out from the spinal cord, passing through small gaps between neighbouring back bones. If the whole backbone is injured, the spinal cord and nerves may get squashed or kinked, resulting in paralysis, numbness and other problems.

the spinal cord

Cervical spinal nerve roots

Cervical part of spinal cord

Rear projection of backbone

Muscle layers of chest

Lumbar part of spinal cord

Brain

Side projection of backbone (vertebra)

Intravertebral blood vessels

Paravertebral ganglion

inside the brain

THE BRAIN IS THE BODY'S CONTROL CENTRE. It is the site of mental processes like thinking and reasoning, imagining and daydreaming, memorizing and remembering, deciding how to behave, and choosing what to do and say. It is the site of the mind, consciousness and awareness. As you read, you process the nerve signals coming from your eyes, recognize the letters and words, recall their meanings, organize them into phrases and sentences, and understand their meaning – all in your brain, using the tiny electrical pulses of nerve signals.

Yet if you cut open a brain, it does not seem to have much of an internal structure. There are a few shadowy parts and groups of fibres, but little else to see. However, modern research is showing that the brain has an amazingly complex inner structure. Research also shows that, although some processes take place in particular parts of the brain, other processes seem to have no one special place or centre.

cutaway brain

Apart from parts at the front and the back, this brain is cut straight down the middle – a slice between the eyes. Luckily it's a model, but it shows many of the brain's main features. The wrinkled cerebral cortex folds around each hemisphere and down towards the middle. There is a slight gap between the two hemispheres, like halves of a walnut. Below the cortex is the corpus callosum, a bridge of 100 million nerve fibres which links the two halves.

Those little grey cells

The most obvious parts of a human brain are the two large, domed, wrinkled bits on top – the cerebral hemispheres. Each has an inner, white portion made mainly from axons (nerve cell "wires") and an outer, grey layer which contains billions of nerve cell bodies, dendrites and axon endings. This is the grey matter, or cerebral cortex, and it's where most of our thinking, reasoning and conscious awareness happen. Different patches of the cerebral cortex, known as centres, deal with signals from the eyes, ears, skin and tongue. Other centres send out nerve signals, telling the muscles to contract and move the body.

brain centres

As you look at an object, signals from your eyes are processed in the sight centre of the brain, so that you can recognize what you see. Taste signals from your tongue are dealt with mainly by the brain's taste centre, and so on.

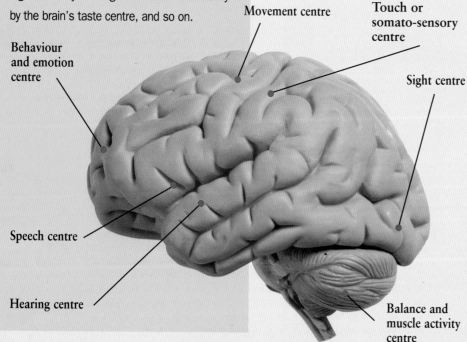

Movement centre

Touch or somato-sensory centre

Behaviour and emotion centre

Sight centre

Speech centre

Hearing centre

Balance and muscle activity centre

Control centre

Under the front of the brain is a part called the hypothalamus, about the size of a small grape. It is the brain's centre for controlling basic processes and urges such as hunger, thirst, sexual desire,

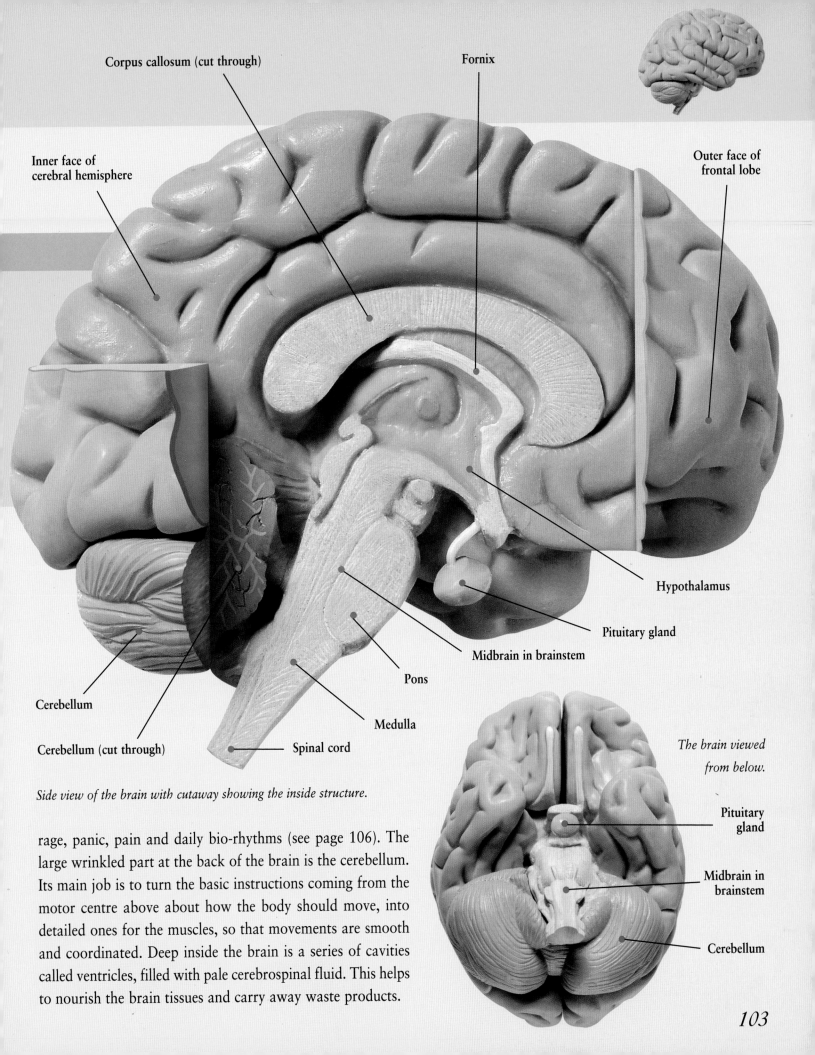

Corpus callosum (cut through)

Fornix

Inner face of
cerebral hemisphere

Outer face of
frontal lobe

Hypothalamus

Pituitary gland

Midbrain in brainstem

Pons

Medulla

Cerebellum

Cerebellum (cut through)

Spinal cord

Side view of the brain with cutaway showing the inside structure.

*The brain viewed
from below.*

Pituitary
gland

Midbrain in
brainstem

Cerebellum

rage, panic, pain and daily bio-rhythms (see page 106). The
large wrinkled part at the back of the brain is the cerebellum.
Its main job is to turn the basic instructions coming from the
motor centre above about how the body should move, into
detailed ones for the muscles, so that movements are smooth
and coordinated. Deep inside the brain is a series of cavities
called ventricles, filled with pale cerebrospinal fluid. This helps
to nourish the brain tissues and carry away waste products.

limits of the mind

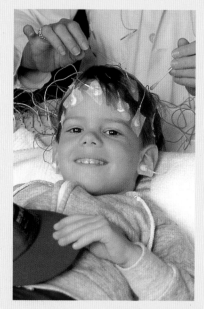

Having an EEG is not painful. It's fun to see your own brain waves!

EVEN WHILE YOU SLEEP, your brain is very busy. We know this from the evidence of "brain waves". As nerve signals whizz around the brain, they send "electrical ripples" through the skull bones to the skin of the head. Sensitive electrodes attached to the skin can pick up these faint signals, to be amplified and displayed as wavy lines on a TV screen or strip of paper. The machine that does this is called an electro-encephalograph, or EEG machine, and the resulting trace is an electro-encephalogram or EEG. There are different shapes or rhythms of wave, depending on whether the person is resting, daydreaming, worried or anxious, or thinking hard. The waves even continue during sleep.

This is just as well. Basic life processes such as heartbeat, breathing, blood pressure, coughing and swallowing are controlled by the brain. If it went to sleep and stopped working, then breathing and heartbeat would cease, and the body would die. The nerve signals controlling these activities go to the muscles concerned from sites, or centres, in the medulla, the lowest part of the base of the brain, where it joins to the spinal cord.

two-sided brain

Each hemisphere, or half, of the cerebral cortex works slightly differently, carrying out the major part of a process such as creating a work of art or thinking through a tricky problem. The two sides of the brain are kept in communication by the corpus callosum, which is a bridge-like set of 100 million nerve fibres (axons) carrying nerve signals between the halves. The differences in cerebral dominance develop from birth to about 12 years of age.

Half a brain

On the outside, and even on the inside, the left half of the brain looks like the right half. But the two halves are not identical in the way they work. For complicated processes such as choosing and speaking words, having ideas and solving problems, one half usually takes the lead. We say that this leading side is dominant. For example, in most people, the centres in the left side of the brain take over when thinking of what to say, and in telling the muscles of the chest, neck, voicebox, throat, mouth and lips how to produce and pronounce the words.

bio-rhythms and the body clock

When you get jet lag, your body's internal clock is set to one time, but the conditions around you are showing a different time. External cycles like daylight and darkness, meal times, working hours, and going to sleep suddenly do not fit. Jet lag may produce drowsiness, headaches and confusion. The problem usually clears up after a few days, as the body clock re-sets itself to its new surroundings. The body clock is based in two tiny groups of a few thousand nerve cells near the hypothalamus, the supra-chiasmatic nuclei. Even when these cells are grown in isolation in a laboratory dish, they show a 24-hour cycle of activity.

This view of the brain from the top shows the two distinct halves, or cerebral hemispheres. The narrow top of this picture is the front of your head.

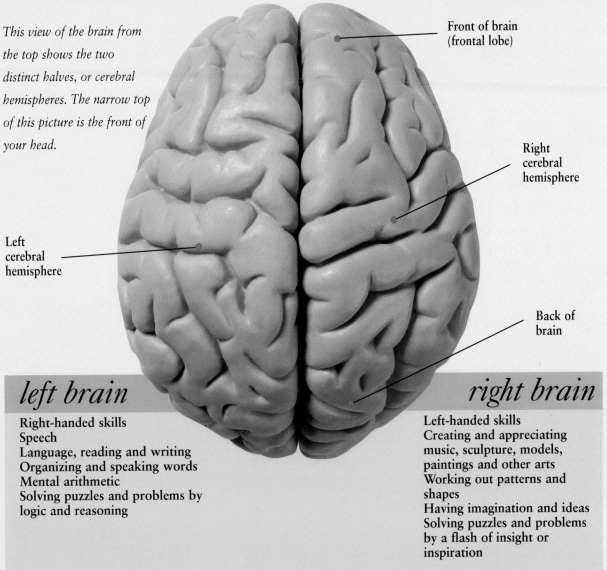

Front of brain (frontal lobe)

Right cerebral hemisphere

Left cerebral hemisphere

Back of brain

left brain

Right-handed skills
Speech
Language, reading and writing
Organizing and speaking words
Mental arithmetic
Solving puzzles and problems by
logic and reasoning

right brain

Left-handed skills
Creating and appreciating
music, sculpture, models,
paintings and other arts
Working out patterns and
shapes
Having imagination and ideas
Solving puzzles and problems
by a flash of insight or
inspiration

24-hour clock

The body has a natural 24-hour cycle of activity. Some of the obvious effects of this are feeling hungry and eating, and feeling tired and going to sleep. There are also many inner cycles or rhythms, such as changes in the levels of blood chemicals and hormones (see page 108). A few years ago, it was discovered that these bio-rhythms are based in two tiny parts of the brain smaller than a baked bean, called the supra-chiasmatic nuclei. They are like the body's biological clock. When people travel by jet to a faraway place, the body suddenly finds that its own rhythms do not fit in with its surroundings. This may cause jet lag.

People who relax through deep meditation can change their brain waves at will.

105

the automatic body

I F YOU HAD TO REMEMBER to do everything, you would not last long! Make your heart beat, now breathe in, then make your heart beat again, squeeze food through the intestines, make another heartbeat... your mind could never keep up. This does not matter, because the brain controls all these processes automatically. It sends out signals along nerves to the muscles in the heart, chest, stomach, intestines and other internal organs, instructing them on when and how to move. You are not aware of all this, unless something unusual happens, like your heart misses a beat in surprise or your breathing becomes fast and shallow as you pant with fear.

The automatic parts of the brain send out many of their signals along a network of nerves called the autonomic nervous system. This works alongside the usual network shown on page 100, which is the peripheral nervous system. The autonomic nerves run to and between the main internal organs like the heart, stomach, intestines, liver, pancreas, kidneys and bladder. They ensure that processes such as digestion, respiration and circulation happen continuously and smoothly.

Running on automatic pilot

The body has other automatic workings, too. When you touch something dangerous – too hot, too cold or very sharp – you jerk away from it almost before you realize it. Nerve signals from the skin, warning you of the hazard, pass along nerves to the spinal cord. At once, nerve signals go back out again to the muscles which move the body part and pull it away. At the same time, more nerve signals go up the spinal cord to the brain, so that you become aware of what's going on. But your body part has already moved. You were not able to stop it, because your brain didn't know. This type of automatic reaction is called a reflex. It is designed mainly to protect the body from dangers by acting instantly, without decisions coming from the brain, which may have its attention elsewhere.

a bundle of reflexes

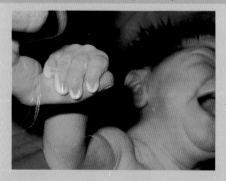

New babies have not learned how to control their arms, legs and other body parts. They move around at random. The main movements are reflexes – fast, automatic responses to something that happens to the body, such as a touch on a certain part. Put something in a new baby's hand, touching the skin there, and the baby will hold it by the grasping reflex. The baby does not yet understand what it is doing or why. But this reflex helps it to cling to its mother or other carer. Similarly, touch a baby's cheek and it turns to that side and tries to suck something. This is called the rooting reflex and it helps the baby to feed from its mother's breast. When its bladder and bowel are full, the baby empties them as reflex actions. Gradually, the baby becomes aware of its movements and learns to control them.

Brain

Even as you sleep, millions of nerve signals flash around the sleeping brain.

Senses

The eyes are closed, but the ears continue to pick up sounds, which the brain screens to see if it needs to wake up.

Breathing

Breathing rate is slow and shallow. There may be a deep breath occasionally to clear the lungs of stale air.

Circulation

The heart never stops. It usually beats more slowly at night since the body is resting.

Digestion

The intestines keep squeezing food through them and mixing it with juices and enzymes.

Even while the body sleeps, its nerve systems are active, continuously monitoring and adjusting the internal processes, and checking the outside world for danger.

the auto-network

There are two main sets of nerves in the autonomic nervous system, and they work in "push–pull" fashion. The parasympathetic nerves tend to make the body calm and relaxed, and slow down processes such as digestion and heartbeat. The sympathetic ones speed up all these processes and activities, so that the body can spring into action. Between them, the two nerve sets fine-tune the body's internal conditions.

signals by chemicals

IN THE TASKS OF CONTROLLING THE BODY and coordinating the activities of its many parts and organs, the brain and nerves do not work on their own. They are assisted by another body system. This works not by tiny electrical nerve signals but by chemicals. These are called hormones, and the system is called the hormonal, or endocrine, system. There are dozens of body hormones. Some have been described already (see page 72), helping to control the body's balance of water, salts and minerals. Others are involved in the way that cells use and store energy, in digestion, in dealing with stress, in growing and maturing from a child to an adult, and in sex and having a baby.

Making hormones

Hormones are made in glands known as endocrine glands. There are about a dozen main endocrine glands – in the head, neck and central body. Specialized cells in the gland make that gland's hormone. Some glands have several sets of specialized cells and produce several different hormones. In general, hormones are quite small molecules. They pass from the cells into the blood flowing through the gland, and are carried around the body in the bloodstream.

hormone-making glands

Some endocrine glands make just one hormone. Others produce several. A few organs or glands have other jobs too. For example, the endocrine parts of the pancreas make two main hormones – insulin and glucagon. The other parts of the pancreas produce enzymes and juices for digestion.

The body's chemical messengers

Hormones travel around the entire body, but each hormone affects only certain parts, called its target tissues and organs. The targets are especially sensitive to the size, shape and other features of their hormone molecule. When they are exposed to it, they respond in some way, such as speeding up their chemical processes. So the hormone carries a message to the target organs or tissues that tells them to "work faster (or slower)". This is why hormones are sometimes called "the body's chemical messengers". The higher the level of hormone in the body, the stronger the message and the greater the response. As various body processes follow the instructions of their hormones, and speed up (or slow down), the results are monitored by sensing centres, especially in the brain. These check that all is well. If something is not right, the sensing centres detect it, and send out their own messages, either along nerves or by other hormones to the glands involved. This continual checking and adjusting is called feedback. So the nerve and hormone systems work together to coordinate the whole body. Nerves work over short time periods, from fractions of a second to minutes. Hormones work over a longer time, from minutes to hours, days and years.

insulin

In some people, the pancreas cannot make the hormone insulin. This means that blood glucose (sugar) is not controlled properly and its levels rise. It "spills over" into the urine, making the urine very copious. So the person has to drink lots of liquids and has little energy, among other problems. This condition is called diabetes mellitus. It can be treated by eating certain foods and/or taking tablets and/or having injections of insulin to replace the missing hormone.

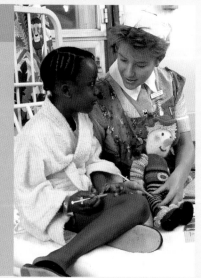

Thyroid

Shaped like a bow tie under the skin of the neck, the thyroid manufactures three main hormones. Calcitonin controls the level of calcium minerals in the blood and bones. Thyroxine and tri-iodothyronine affect blood pressure and the speed of general body chemistry.

Parathyroid

These four mini-glands, stuck onto the thyroid, produce parathyroid hormone, which helps to control body minerals, mainly calcium.

Adrenal

The outer cortex layer, makes hormones for fluid balance, resisting stress and sexual reproduction. The inner medulla produces adrenaline and noradrenaline (see right).

Kidneys

Renin from the kidneys is involved in water and salt balance (see page 72). Another of its hormones – erythropoietin – speeds red blood cell manufacture by bone marrow.

Pituitary

This tiny gland under the brain is the "master" of the hormone system. It receives messages from the hypothalamus and other brain parts and sends out at least 10 hormones, including growth hormones and hormones that control the thyroid and adrenals.

Stomach

Several hormones from the stomach affect digestion, including the activity of the intestines and the stomach itself.

Pancreas

Insulin and glucagon control the level of blood glucose (sugar) and the way body cells use this energy source.

Sex glands

These are the ovaries in a woman and the testes in a man. Their workings and hormones, called sex hormones, are explained in the next chapter.

did you know?

IN AN EMOTIONAL, STRESSFUL OR SCARY SITUATION, YOUR BODY REACTS BY THE FIGHT-OR-FLIGHT RESPONSE. IT IS CONTROLLED BY NERVES AND BY ADRENAL HORMONES ADRENALINE AND NORADRENALINE.

➤ HEART BEATS HARDER, FASTER.

➤ LUNGS BREATHE FASTER, MORE DEEPLY.

➤ LIVER RELEASES STORES OF GLUCOSE INTO BLOOD AS ENERGY FOR MUSCLES.

➤ MUSCLES BECOME TENSE AND READY FOR ACTION.

chapter

7

THERE'S A TINY NEW BABY, fast asleep. Aaaah! Oh no, she's woken up and started crying. Aarrgh! We all begin life as new-born babies. But in fact, a new human being really begins nine months earlier than this. A microscopic sperm

reproduction

cell from the father joins with an egg cell from the mother, to make one new cell – the fertilized egg, or zygote – that is smaller than the dot on this i. From such tiny beginnings, the cell multiplies into many cells, and a miniature human body begins to

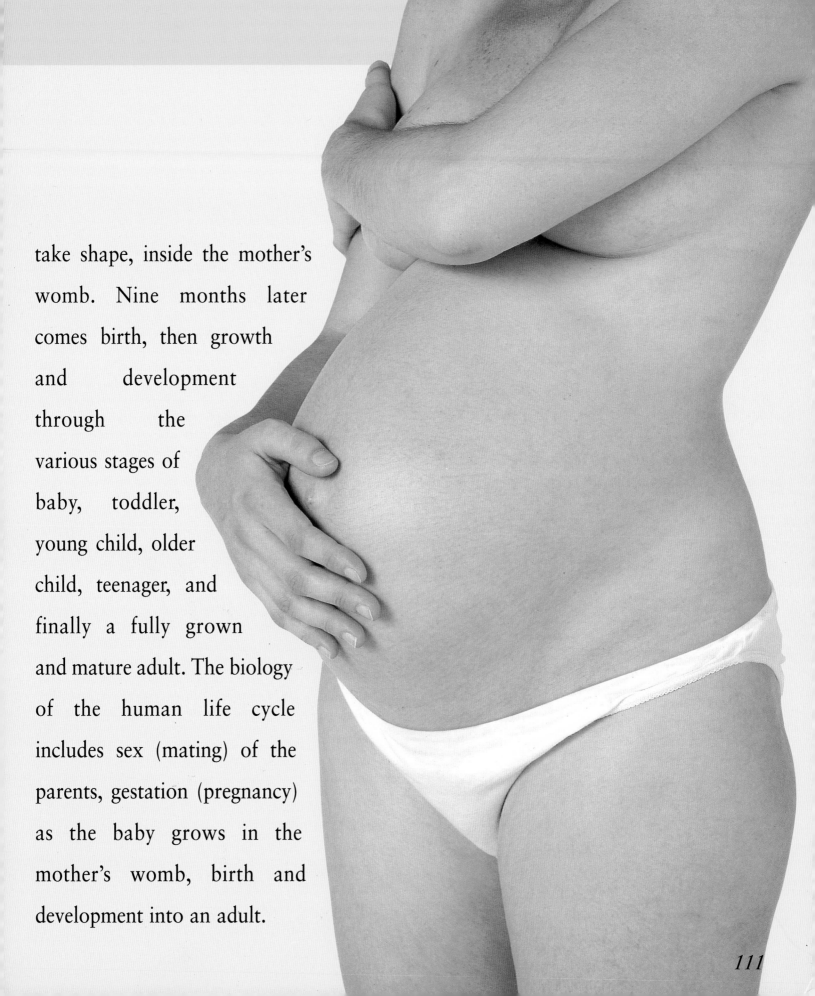

take shape, inside the mother's womb. Nine months later comes birth, then growth and development through the various stages of baby, toddler, young child, older child, teenager, and finally a fully grown and mature adult. The biology of the human life cycle includes sex (mating) of the parents, gestation (pregnancy) as the baby grows in the mother's womb, birth and development into an adult.

the female parts

THERE ARE TWO MAIN KINDS of human body – male and female. The parts of the body involved in reproduction are called the sex organs. The main female sex organs are the ovaries, uterus (womb) and vagina. The ovaries are two glands shaped like hen's eggs, in the sides of the lower abdomen. Their jobs are to make hormones and also to ripen and release their human eggs, which are single but giant cells, each slightly smaller than a pinhead. A mature woman has about 10,000 egg cells, or ova, in her two ovaries. However, these are not properly developed, or ripe. Usually, one egg cell ripens every 28 days, in alternate ovaries. This process happens under control of sex hormones, as part of the regular female bodily changes called the menstrual cycle (see panel below).

How the female body works

The ripe egg pops out of the ovary into a tube known as the oviduct, or fallopian tube. It wafts through this, propelled by the waving action of micro-hairs – cilia – that line it. If the egg cell meets a sperm cell in the oviduct, it may be fertilized (see page 116). The female body then nourishes the fertilized egg as it develops into a baby in the womb.

If the egg is not fertilized, it carries on along the oviduct and reaches the chamber, or cavity, inside the uterus. Over the previous few days, the lining of the uterus has grown thick and rich with blood and nutrients, to feed a fertilized egg. But if the egg is not fertilized, the blood-rich uterus lining is not needed. It breaks down and passes, along with the egg cell, through the cervix and the vagina to the outside. This loss of blood and lining is called menstruation, or the period, and usually lasts around four or five days. It may be painful because the muscles which make up the womb wall contract in spasms. After a few more days, the whole menstrual cycle starts again. It means that a woman can conceive – that is, an egg can be fertilized by a sperm – during only a few days in the middle of the cycle. This is called her fertile time.

the female organs

The uterus, or womb, is about the size and shape of a pear, near the base of the abdomen. It is linked to the outside by the vagina, or birth canal. A baby passes along this at birth, from inside the uterus to the outside world. The muscular opening or neck of the womb is the cervix. On either side of the uterus are the ovaries, held in position by ligaments. The tubes called oviducts join each ovary to the uterus, so that a ripe egg can pass to it during the middle of each menstrual cycle.

the menstrual cycle

In many women, this cycle is regular and lasts about 28 days. A typical cycle is shown here. But variations in length, with a few days more or less, are also common. Illness, drastic weight loss and strong emotional events can disrupt the cycle.

Days 1–4	Blood and uterus lining lost through vagina (the period)
Days 5–14	Lining of uterus thickens and becomes blood-rich
Day 14	Ovulation – ripe egg released from ovary
Days 12–16	Usual fertile time (but can vary)
Days 15–28	Uterus lining stays thick and blood-rich

main hormones of the cycle

FSH (Follicle stimulating hormone) Made in the pituitary gland near the brain. Makes an egg cell ripen in its sac-like container or follicle.

Oestrogen Made in the ripening follicle in the ovary. Encourages the uterus lining to become thicker and blood-rich. Also produces general female features of the body.

LH (Luteinizing hormone) Made in the pituitary gland. Causes the egg to be released from its follicle and the follicle to become a corpus luteum (see below).

Progesterone Made in the corpus luteum, a small yellow gland that forms from the empty follicle after its egg has gone. It keeps the uterus lining thick and blood-rich.

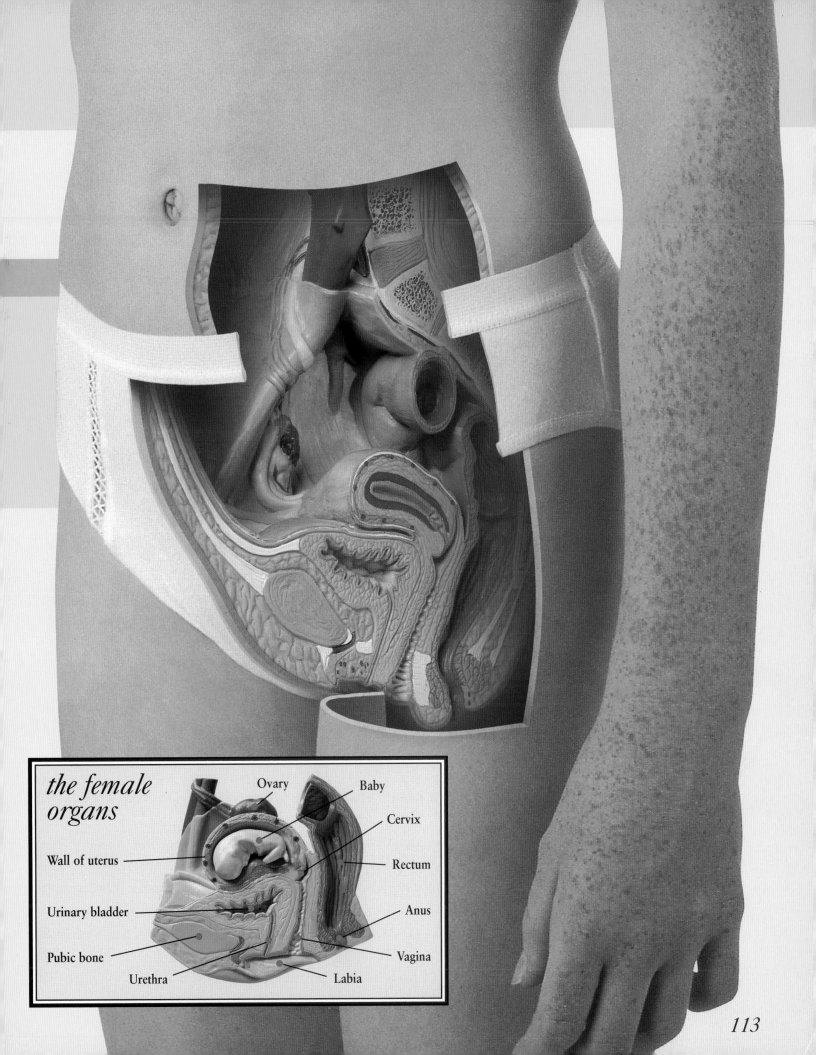

the female organs

Ovary

Baby

Cervix

Wall of uterus

Rectum

Urinary bladder

Anus

Pubic bone

Vagina

Urethra

Labia

the male parts

N THE FEMALE HUMAN BODY, the sex cell is the egg. Its formation happens in a cycle – one egg matures every 28 days. In the male human body, the sex cell is the sperm. But sperm do not ripen one at a time, every 28 days. They are being made all the time, in their millions. The amazing sperm production factory happens in the main male sex organs, the testes (testicles). These hang from the lower abdomen in a skin bag called the scrotum.

Each testis contains a complicated set of folded and coiled tubes – the seminiferous tubules. These are arranged in a fan pattern. Unravelled and joined together, the 1,000 or so tubules from one testis would be about 500 m (550 yds) long. Inside the tubules, cells are continuously multiplying and developing into sperm, at the rate of around 300 million each day. Each sperm is "born" when a germinal cell in the lining of the tubule divides. It takes about six weeks for the sperm cell to grow and mature into its final tadpole-like shape. As it does so, it moves from the edge of the tubule into the middle, with millions of other sperms. All this happens under the influence of the main male hormone, testosterone.

the male organs

Unlike the female sex organs, the male ones are mainly outside the abdomen. Hanging below the main body, the testes are usually a degree or two cooler than the main body temperature of 37 °C (98.4 °F). This helps sperm production, which happens more slowly at 37 °C (98.4 °F). In the male, both sperm and urine pass along the urethra (but not at the same time).

The journey of a sperm

The maturing sperm pass slowly into the epididymis, another set of coiled tubes about 6 m (6 yds) long, attached to the side of the testis. They are stored here for a time. Some also move into the next part of the tube, the sperm duct or vas deferens, which is about 40 cm (16 in) long, where they are stored, too. These millions of sperm, in a milky liquid called seminal fluid, may be squirted out of the other main male sex organ, the penis. This is known as ejaculation. If sperm are not ejaculated, they gradually die and break down, and their parts are taken back into the body, as more sperm are formed daily to replace them.

The penis hangs in front of the scrotum. In reproduction, its main job is to become erect – larger and stiffer. Then it can be pushed inside the female's vagina. This means that when sperm pass along the urethra, the tube inside the penis, they will emerge into the female vagina, near to the uterus. It gives them a better chance of swimming through the cervix and into the uterus and into the oviducts, to fertilize an egg (see page 116).

family planning

Contraception is preventing or stopping the development of a baby, when it might otherwise occur. These are some of various methods, suited to different people and situations.

➤ Barrier methods stop the sperm from reaching the egg. The condom or sheath fits over the man's penis and catches the sperm as they come out.

➤ The diaphragm or cervical cap fits over the neck of the womb and stops sperm passing from the vagina into the uterus.

➤ Chemical methods include spermicides – substances which kill or disable sperm. They can be used along with barrier methods.

➤ Hormonal methods include the various kinds of "pill" (oral contraceptives), injections and under-skin implants. They work mainly by changing the menstrual cycle so that a ripe egg is not released.

➤ The IUD (intra-uterine device) is a small piece of shaped plastic, with a metal or hormone in it. This fits inside the uterus. It prevents a fertilized egg from burrowing into the womb lining and growing there.

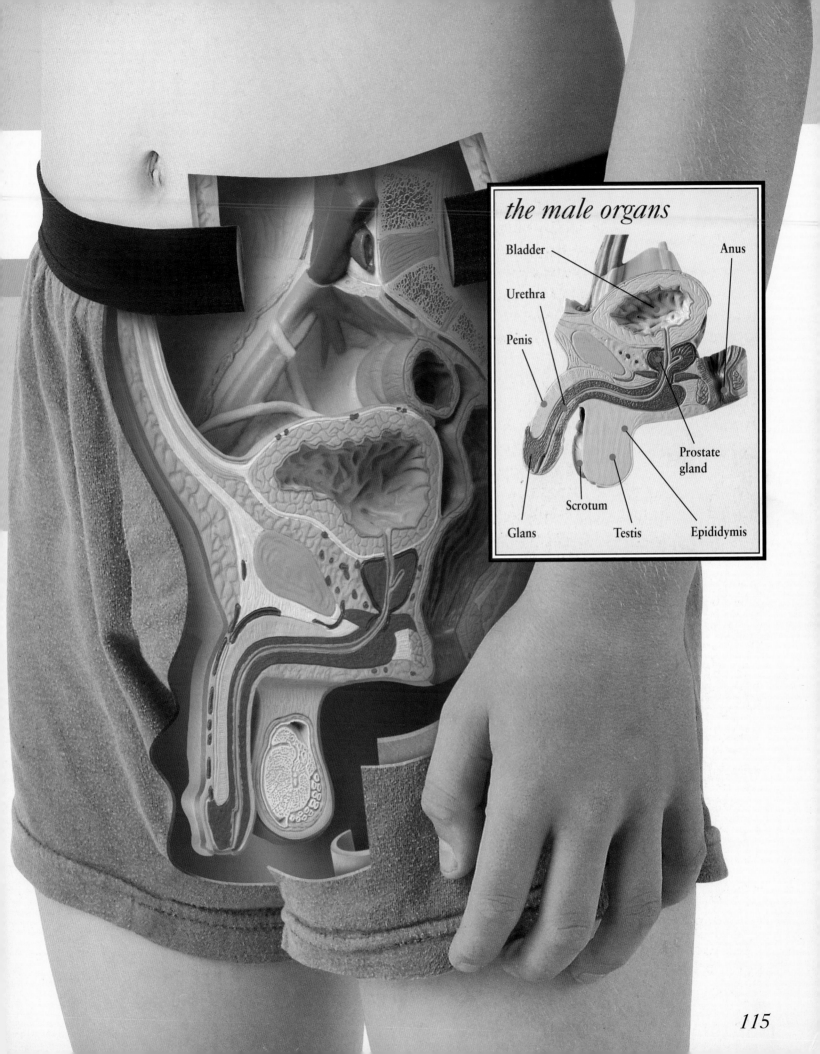

the male organs

Bladder

Anus

Urethra

Penis

Prostate
gland

Glans

Scrotum

Testis

Epididymis

115

a new life begins

A BABY GROWS INSIDE its mother's womb for nine months before it is born. It began as a fertilized egg – a pinhead-sized egg cell from the mother joined with an even smaller tadpole-shaped sperm cell from the father (see page 114). In the oviduct, or fallopian tube, of the mother, sperm swim towards the egg cell. Of the original millions of sperm, many have already died on their way through the female organs. Some go into the other oviduct where there is no egg. In the correct oviduct, thousands may cluster around the ripe egg cell. But only one fertilizes the egg. Once this happens, the fertilized egg forms a barrier around itself to keep out other sperm.

Becoming a baby

The father's genetic material (see page 122) is inside the front part – or head – of the sperm. It is only a half-set of genes, formed by a specialized type of cell division called meiosis that produces sperm (or eggs). When the egg and sperm cells join, the sperm's genetic material enters the much larger egg cell. It takes place with the genetic material already there, a half-set from the mother, formed by a similar meiosis that makes egg cells.

The fertilized egg now has a full set of genes and it can begin to develop from a single ball-shaped cell into the billions of different, specialized and busy cells that make up a human being. The first thing it does, about 25–30 hours after fertilization, is to divide or split in half by mitosis (see page 22), to form two smaller but complete cells. Around 15–20 hours later, each of these cells divides again. And the same thing continues to happen, every few hours. By about five or six days after fertilization, the original single fertilized egg cell has become a blastocyst – a small blackberry-like ball of much smaller cells – but it doesn't look like a baby yet.

egg cell

A typical egg cell is about 120 micrometres (0.12 mm or 0.005 in) across. It has the mother's genetic material in its nucleus, and a hazy layer around it called the zona pellucida. It is usually surrounded by other cells which have come from the ovarian follicle.

sperm cell

The average sperm has a head containing the genetic material, a middle piece containing lots of the energy-converting parts called mitochondria, and a long, whippy tail. The whole sperm is only 50 micrometres (0.05 mm or 0.002 in) long, and most of this is the thin tail.

fertilization

The single sperm that will fertilize the egg noses onto the egg cell's surface. It releases from its front tip a chemical enzyme, called hyaluronidase, which dissolves a small patch of the egg cell's outer membrane. The genetic material inside the sperm's head can now pass through into the egg cell. This is the actual moment of fertilization.

Into the womb

All this time, the blastocyst drifts along the oviduct and into the uterus. It has been living on stored nutrients in the original egg cell. But now it needs new nourishment. So it burrows into the thick, blood-rich lining of the uterus, the endometrium. It "eats" its way in, taking in nutrients from tissues around it. This process is called implantation. From such tiny beginnings,

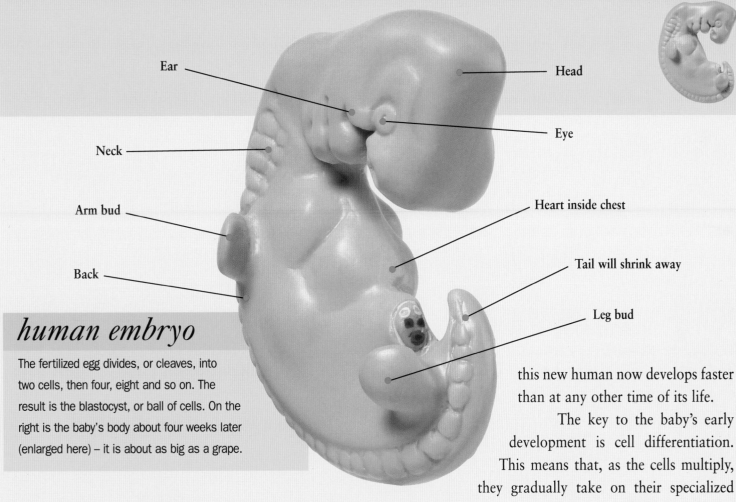

Ear

Head

Eye

Neck

Arm bud

Heart inside chest

Back

Tail will shrink away

Leg bud

human embryo

The fertilized egg divides, or cleaves, into two cells, then four, eight and so on. The result is the blastocyst, or ball of cells. On the right is the baby's body about four weeks later (enlarged here) – it is about as big as a grape.

this new human now develops faster than at any other time of its life.

The key to the baby's early development is cell differentiation. This means that, as the cells multiply, they gradually take on their specialized shapes and jobs, as nerve cells, muscle cells, blood cells and so on. The cells also move, or migrate, taking up their correct places in the tiny body. The instructions for this amazingly complex process are carried in the genes.

Adding the finishing touches

This all happens at the level of molecules and cells. Much of the body's main development happens during the first two months in the uterus. The baby is still only the size of a thumb, yet recognizably human, with a beating heart, eyes and ears, blood, nerves, muscles covered by skin, and bones beginning to harden. To this stage, it is called an embryo.

After two months or so, the baby is known as a fetus. Its main activity is to grow bigger, and add details such as eyelids, fingernails and toenails.

Ovary

Amnion membrane

Muscular wall of uterus

Fetus

Cervix

Three months after fertilization, the fetus is recognizably human.

fertility treatment

About one couple in ten who would like to have a baby are unable to do so because of reproductive problems. Modern medicine can help in various ways. "In vitro" fertilization involves taking ripe egg cells from the mother and sperm cells from the father, mixing them in a test tube so that fertilization can occur, and then putting fertilized eggs back into the mother's womb to continue their development. There are many other types of fertility treatment, such as hormone pills or injections to make the woman's ovaries release extra ripe eggs, for a better chance of fertilization.

into the world

BEFORE THE MICROSCOPE was invented, people believed that the human body began tiny yet fully formed – the complete baby shape, but too small to see. Now we know that the body gradually develops from the blastocyst, a clump of cells that all look the same. It has usually grown strong enough to be born nine months after fertilization. The powerful muscles that make up the wall of the uterus contract strongly, pressing the baby towards the cervix (neck of the womb). The muscles at the cervix relax and the baby is squeezed through the vagina, or birth canal, to the outside world.

The life-support placenta

Inside the uterus, the baby is surrounded by fluid. It cannot breathe for itself or eat. It obtains oxygen and nourishment from its mother through a disc-shaped organ – the placenta – embedded in the womb wall. The baby is linked to the placenta by the umbilical cord, carrying blood to and from its body. In the placenta, blood from the baby passes close to the mother's blood, and absorbs nutrients and oxygen from it. Then blood then flows back along the cord to the baby's body.

Being born

After the baby has been born, the placenta (or afterbirth) comes away from the womb wall and follows through the birth canal. The baby takes its first gasps of air, perhaps crying to open the air passages and clear them of fluid and mucus. The birth process may take 12 hours or more for a first-time mother. It is very tiring for both baby and mother, and they rest together, getting to know each other and becoming used to new sights, sounds and smells. The baby may take some milk from the mother's breast – its first feed. It is one of the most magical moments of any life.

five months to go

Four months of development have seen the baby pass through the stage where it is a flat disc of cells, then a worm-like shape, then gradually taking on human form. The limbs begin as flaps growing from the body, which lengthen and become shaped into arms and legs. Now they are developing nails on the fingers and toes. At this stage the baby is about 10–12 cm (4–5 in) long. This baby is lying sideways in the womb, and this position is called the transverse position.

the baby in its mother

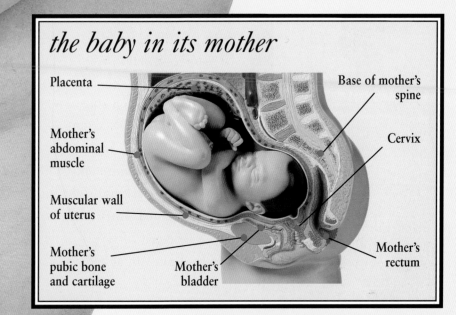

Placenta

Base of mother's spine

Mother's abdominal muscle

Cervix

Muscular wall of uterus

Mother's pubic bone and cartilage

Mother's bladder

Mother's rectum

ultrasound

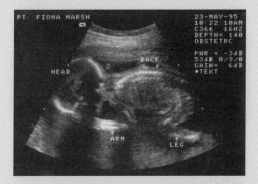

PT: FIONA MARSH
23-MAY-95
10:22:10AM
C366 16HZ
DEPTH= 140
OBSTETRC

PWR = -3dB
53dB 0/3/0
GAIN= 6dB
*TEXT

BACK

HEAD

ARM

LEG

In some countries, expectant mothers receive check-ups to make sure that they are healthy and the baby is developing normally. One check is the ultrasound scan, usually taken at 15–20 weeks. Harmless, very high-pitched sound waves, undetectable by our ears, are beamed through the mother's body. The waves reflect off fluid, skin, muscles and bones in different ways. The probe picks up the echoes, which are analysed by computer and displayed on a screen. The resulting image of the baby in the uterus can be used to check the baby's heart, brain and other organs – and to see if it's a boy or girl.

growing up

THE HUMAN BODY PASSES THROUGH many stages of development. During the early years these tend to involve mainly physical skills of movement and coordination. The stages usually happen in the same order, though the exact timings are more variable. Most babies can sit up before they can crawl, and crawl before they can walk. Occasionally a baby misses a stage, or reaches one early or late. This rarely signifies anything important. However in most countries, babies and children receive regular check-ups from health workers or doctors. These generally include taking height and weight measurements, assessing motor skills (movement and coordination) such as the ability to put bricks into the correct-shaped holes, and checking sight, hearing, heartbeat, breathing and other body functions. These tests are designed to reveal problems, so that they can be dealt with at an early stage.

Going to school

In the later years, development shifts to the mental arena. We attend school for 10 years or more. We begin with reading, writing and arithmetic. Then we learn about more advanced topics such as other languages, branches of mathematics, humanities, science, art and music. Many children sample a variety of sports, games and pastimes. They may develop great enthusiasm and skill, in areas from chess to cross-country running to computer games.

Being a person

And all the time, often without realizing, we are experiencing and learning about life in general. In biological terms, the human species *Homo sapiens* is grouped with the great apes, chimpanzees and gorillas, in the large group called primates. The vast majority of these are social rather than solitary, living in groups and having many relationships. Some anthropologists study primate social behaviour and consider how – or if – it can be applied to the human being which, it is readily admitted, is a vastly more complex animal.

Around the age of 10 years, physical development enters a rapid growth phase.

developmental stages

Most children develop physical and mental skills in the same order, but not at exactly the same time. The timings listed here are average times. Many babies and children reach these developmental stages earlier or later. And usually this has no effect on future development, or life in general.

- **6 weeks** Smile
- **3 months** Lift head and shoulders from face-down position
- **5 months** Roll over from lying face-down
- **7 months** After being helped to sit up, stay there almost unassisted
- **7 months** Make "baby babble" noises with no particular meaning
- **8 months** Sit up unassisted
- **10 months** Crawl well with straight arms
- **12 months** Stand up for a short time
- **15 months** Walk unaided
- **18 months** Say simple words at the appropriate time with meaning and understanding
- **20–24 months** Control bowel movements
- **24 months** Put words together into simple sentences
- **24–28 months** Control urination during the day
- **36–48 months** Control urination during the night

breast is best

Like all new-born mammals, the baby human thrives on its mother's milk. It contains the right nutrients at the right temperature, and also antibodies which help to protect against infection. However, the views on this most basic of mammalian activities vary enormously around the world, according to local custom. They have also changed with time, according to fashions. And they are affected by individual circumstances, such as health problems, or mothers who work. Some babies are bottle-fed from the beginning. Some are weaned from mother's milk onto foods by four months, while others by about one year. In some areas children are still being breastfed at the age of three or four years.

In the family, then with friends and at playgroups, young children learn about behaviour patterns, what is acceptable and what's not, being "good" and "naughty", and developing relationships. At school, there is a social education too. Friends form groups, with the trials and tribulations of the playground, loyalties and shifting allegiances, peer pressure, bullying, meeting girlfriends and boyfriends, team cooperation, and many other formative experiences.

- **4–5 years** Hop and skip. Further development tends to depend on the amount and type of teaching or schooling, for example:
- **5 years** Read simple sentences
- **5–6 years** Draw a human-type figure with separate head, body and limbs
- **6 years** Write simple sentences

Into adulthood

The teenage years of puberty and adolescence give way to adulthood. Most human bodies are fully physically mature by about 20 years of age. Yet many people are still developing social and behavioural skills. They may adopt or adapt or reject their local traditions and customs, perhaps replacing them with a new set of ideas and practices. The "wisdom of age", based on decades of experience and observation, is still many years in the future.

the body in the future

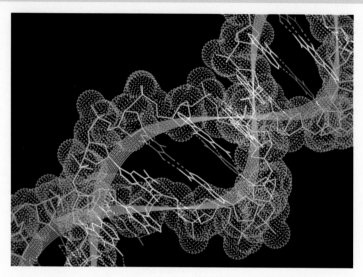

This computer image of DNA shows two inter-wound strands (blue) linked by pairs of subunit bases: guanine (G) and adenine (A) in yellow, and thymine (D) and cytosine (C) in red.

N 1953 TWO SCIENTISTS, Francis Crick and James Watson, discovered the structure of DNA, the "molecule of life". Along its length, DNA has patterns of four subunits (see Glossary), represented by the letters A, T, G and C. The order of the subunits varies – and that is the key. It's like varying the order of the letters in the alphabet when you write out words and sentences. So DNA is a chemical version of a written instruction book, although the DNA alphabet has only four letters, not 26 like our English alphabet.

The whole "DNA book" contains the information for building and running a living thing. Each and every type of living organism – an amoeba, a gnat, a seaweed, a daisy, an oak tree, a human being like you – has its own DNA book.

A gene is like a sentence in the book. It gives an instruction on how to build one of the thousands of molecules in the body, such as the protein keratin in the skin, or the haemoglobin molecule in red blood cells. In total, there are probably between 100,000 and 200,000 genes in the DNA book for a human body. These are not strung along one enormously long DNA molecule. They are packaged like the separate volumes which make up one multi-volume book. Each "volume" of DNA is called a chromosome, a tiny thread-like structure inside the nucleus of a cell.

How DNA gets into every cell

There are 46 chromosomes in the full human set: 23 came from the mother and were in the egg cell, and 23 came from the father in the sperm cell. Every time a cell divides by the process of mitosis (see page 22), every piece of DNA in every chromosome is copied. This means that each cell in the body has, inside its nucleus, the entire set of 46 chromosomes, containing all 100,000–200,000 genes. Cells become different in their shapes, activities, functions and products because only some of their genes are switched on and working. A few types of cell, like red blood cells, have lost their nuclei and do not have any genes. However, when sperm and egg cells form, they do so by another type of cell division known as meiosis (see page 116).

translating the book

Today, scientists are busy translating the entire "instruction book" of genes, which are in the form of the chemical DNA. It's a worldwide project coordinated by HUGO, the Human Genome Organization (a genome is the full set, or complement, of genes for a living thing). Scientists are also working on ways of indentifying genes that cause problems such as illness. More than 100 diseases, such as muscular dystrophy, are known to be caused by faulty genes. And many others, such as breast cancer, are linked to certain types of gene.

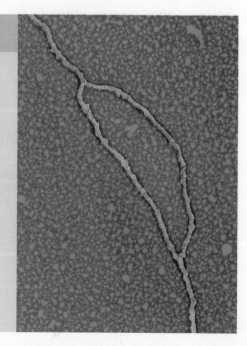

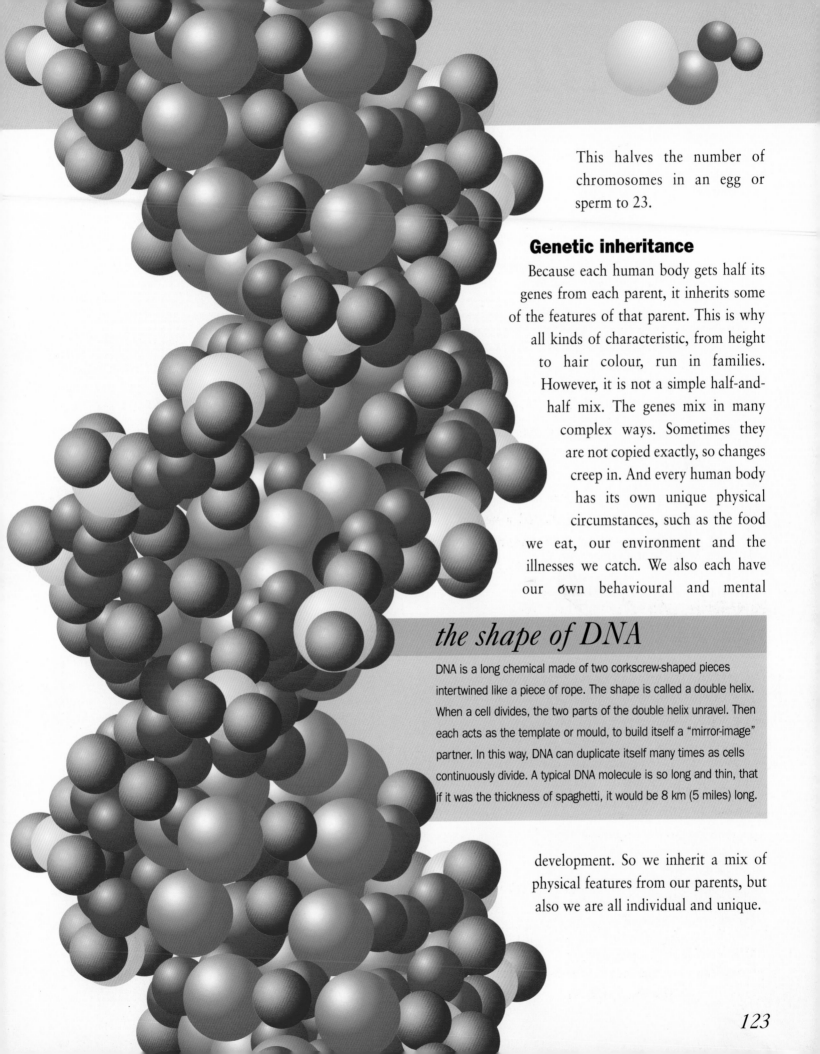

This halves the number of chromosomes in an egg or sperm to 23.

Genetic inheritance

Because each human body gets half its genes from each parent, it inherits some of the features of that parent. This is why all kinds of characteristic, from height to hair colour, run in families. However, it is not a simple half-and-half mix. The genes mix in many complex ways. Sometimes they are not copied exactly, so changes creep in. And every human body has its own unique physical circumstances, such as the food we eat, our environment and the illnesses we catch. We also each have our own behavioural and mental

the shape of DNA

DNA is a long chemical made of two corkscrew-shaped pieces intertwined like a piece of rope. The shape is called a double helix. When a cell divides, the two parts of the double helix unravel. Then each acts as the template or mould, to build itself a "mirror-image" partner. In this way, DNA can duplicate itself many times as cells continuously divide. A typical DNA molecule is so long and thin, that if it was the thickness of spaghetti, it would be 8 km (5 miles) long.

development. So we inherit a mix of physical features from our parents, but also we are all individual and unique.

glossary

This glossary explains words that appear in the rest of the book. Words in italics have glossary entries of their own.

ANTIBODY A tiny particle made by the body in response to infection. Antibodies stick onto or attack invading germs and other foreign objects.

AORTA The largest, thickest blood vessel. It is the main *artery* that carries oxygen-rich blood from the left side of the heart, and splits into many branches to supply the whole body.

ARTERY A large, thick-walled, strong blood vessel that carries blood away from the heart under high pressure. An artery branches many times to form *capillaries*.

ATOM The smallest part of a substance that can exist and still have the chemical features of that substance – a single particle of a chemical element. Atoms join together to make *molecules*. Atoms are made up of smaller particles such as electrons, protons and neutrons.

ATRIUM In the heart, one of the two thin-walled upper chambers, also called auricles, which receive blood from the veins. Also, the name of the outer ear – the ear flap on the side of the head.

CALORIE See *joule*.

CAPILLARY The smallest blood vessel, finer than a hair, and usually less than 1 mm long. There are millions all over the body. They form from branched *arteries* and join to make *veins*.

CARDIOVASCULAR To do with the heart (*cardio-*) and the network of blood vessels, the circulatory or blood-vascular system.

CARTILAGE Another word for "gristle" – a pale, pearly, smooth, slightly squishy and very hard-wearing substance. It works as a shock-absorber and friction-reducer in joints, and also forms the bendy framework of parts like the ear, nose and voice-box.

CELL The basic unit of all life. A germ such as a bacterium is one cell. The human body has billions of cells of many different kinds. An average cell is 20–30 micrometres across. About 40 in a line would stretch 1 mm.

CEREBELLUM The smallish, wrinkled part at the lower rear of the brain. It helps to control muscles and make movements smooth and coordinated.

CIRCULATION Anything that goes round and round. In the body, the main circulation is of blood through the heart and blood vessels. *Lymph* also circulates, as does cerebrospinal fluid inside the brain.

CORONARY To do with the blood vessels that carry blood to the muscles of the heart, which make up the heart wall. A "coronary" is the name used for a type of heart attack, when one or more coronary arteries becomes blocked.

DIURETIC A substance such as a medical drug that encourages the body to make more urine, usually to get rid of extra water or body salts.

DNA De-oxyribonucleic acid, the huge molecule that is shaped like a double helix (corkscrew). It carries, as chemical codes, the *genes* needed to make and run the human body.

ENDOCRINE SYSTEM The hormonal glands and the *hormones* they make, which control many longer-term body processes and activities, such as growth, levels of glucose sugar in the blood, the female menstrual cycle and pregnancy.

ENZYME A type of chemical that speeds up (or slows down) changes in other chemicals. There are thousands of enzymes in the body's cells and tissues, each controlling a certain chemical reaction.

EXCRETION Getting rid of wastes, by-products and other unwanted or excess substances. The main excretory parts of the body are the kidneys (making urine), liver (losing unwanted salts and chemicals), skin (losing water and salt) and lungs (losing carbon dioxide and water).

GENE An instruction or "blueprint" for making a certain part of the body, or instructing how that part works. Genes are codes for proteins in the form of *DNA*. The human body has about 100,000–200,000 genes.

GLUCOSE The simplest type of sugar, chemical formula $C_6H_{12}O_6$. It comes from digested food, circulates in the blood as "blood sugar" and is the body's main source of energy to power its life processes.

HAEMOGLOBIN A substance in red blood cells that "likes" oxygen. It attaches to oxygen in the lungs and carries it to all body parts for use in cellular *respiration*. There are about 270 million molecules of haemoglobin in each red blood cell.

HOMEOSTASIS The condition of "staying the same". It is the general name for the many processes that keep conditions inside the body fairly constant, such as its temperature, amounts of water and concentrations of various chemicals.

HOMO SAPIENS "Wise human", the official scientific name for the human species. It includes all human beings alive today.

HORMONE A chemical made by an *endocrine* gland, which circulates in the blood and controls a body process. The hormones insulin and glucagon, made in the pancreas, control the amount of glucose sugar that is in the blood and available as energy.

HYPOTHALAMUS A small part at the lower front of the brain. It deals with basic body instincts and urges such as hunger and thirst, emotions like fear, pleasure and anger, also sexual feelings and automatic body processes such as digestion and body temperature.

IMMUNE DEFENCE SYSTEM The system that defends the body against invading "germs" and other infecting microbes, and various other forms of disease and illness, including some cancers. It involves parts throughout the body, such as white blood cells, lymph nodes ("glands") and the thymus. One of its defence methods is to make *antibodies*.

IMMUNIZATION The process of becoming immune or protected.

INOCULATION To put a *vaccine* or similar substance into the body, to give immunity and protect against infection. It may be done by injection or pricking into the skin.

JOULE The scientific unit of energy, or work. A resting human body uses about 3–5 kJ (kilojoules or 1,000 joules) each minute. Energy contents of foods are given as kJ on their packets. An older unit is the Calorie (kcal or 1,000 calories). 4.2 kJ = 1 Calorie.

LIGAMENT A tough, stretchy, strap-like part that links the bones in a joint. It stops the joint coming apart or bending too far.

LYMPH A pale fluid that collects between cells and flows slowly in tubes called lymph vessels around the body. It eventually joins the blood system.

MAMMAL A large group of about 4,000 kinds, or species, of animal. A typical mammal is a *vertebrate*, is warm-blooded, has fur or hair, and the female feeds her babies on milk. Bats, rats, cats, dogs, hogs, whales, seals, kangaroos and humans are all mammals.

MEMBRANE A thin, bag-like "skin" that covers or lines something. A cell membrane is like a bag around a single *cell*. The buccal membrane covers the inside of the cheek.

MENSTRUATION The periodic flow of blood from the womb (uterus) of certain female mammals, including humans. It is part of the menstrual, or reproductive, cycle and is also called the period.

METABOLISM The general name for the thousands of chemical changes and reactions that occur in the body, second by second.

MINERAL A mineral is an inorganic substance needed for growth and health. Minerals play a vital role in regulating many body functions. Minerals are usually chemical elements (single chemical substances), such as calcium for strong bones and teeth, and iron for healthy blood.

MOLECULE Two or more *atoms* joined together. Oxygen gas in the air is a very small molecule of two oxygen atoms, O_2. *DNA* is a gigantic molecule made up of many thousands of different atoms.

MUSCLE A body *tissue* specialized to get shorter, or contract. The body has over 600 muscles to move its bones (skeletal muscles), as well as muscle in its heart, intestines and other internal organs (cardiac and visceral muscle).

NUTRIENT Any substance that the body needs for growth, life processes, maintenance and repair usually taken in as food or drink.

ORGAN A main part of the body that does one major job, such as the heart, lung, brain, liver or intestine.

PERISTALSIS Waves of muscle action that push substances along inside a body tube. This includes swallowed food moving in the gullet (oesophagus), digested food in the intestines, urine in the ureter and egg cells in the oviduct (fallopian tube).

PLASMA The pale yellow fluid that makes up about half the volume of blood. It contains hundreds of dissolved substances, including sugars, salts, minerals and hormones.

PRIMATE The group of *mammals* to which humans belong. It also includes apes like chimps and gorillas, monkeys, lemurs and bushbabies.

PROTEIN A main group of *molecules* found in all living things. Proteins usually form the structural or framework parts of cells, bones, muscles and other body parts. *Enzymes* are also proteins. Healthy food contains plant and/or animal proteins that the body breaks down by digestion and rebuilds into its own parts.

PULMONARY To do with the lungs. For instance, the pulmonary arteries carry low-oxygen blood to the lungs.

RESPIRATION The movements of breathing in and out. Also, the chemical process which releases energy from *glucose* sugar to power a cell's life processes (cellular respiration).

TENDON A strong, tapering, rope-like part at the end of a *muscle*. It joins the muscle firmly to a bone or other part, so that the muscle can pull it.

TISSUE A group, layer or collection of similar cells, all working together. Muscle cells make up muscle tissue, and nerve cells (neurons) make up nerve tissue.

UREA One of the body's main waste products, which comes largely from the breakdown of *proteins*. It is *excreted* in urine.

VACCINATION The process of putting a vaccine in the body to give it protection, or *immunization*, against certain diseases.

VEIN A large, thin-walled, floppy blood vessel that carries blood back to the heart. Veins are formed when many *capillaries* join together.

VENTRICLE In the heart, one of the two thick-walled lower chambers, which pump blood out into the arteries.

VERTEBRATE An animal with a backbone or spinal column, which is a row of bones called vertebrae. The main groups of vertebrates are fish, amphibians, reptiles, birds and mammals – including humans.

index

H

haemoglobin 17, 66, 122, 124
haemophilia 83
hair 12, *13, 26, 27,* 78, 79, 97
hair cells 92, *93,*
hammer bone 90, *93*
Havers, Clopton 30
haversian system 30
hearing 84, 90-91, 92-93, *102*
heart 18, *18,* 56, *57, 61,* 62-63,
    70, *107*
heart disease *63*
heart muscle *41*
heartbeat 62, *62;* 104
    rate 63, 65
hepatic artery 77, *77*
hepatic lobules 76
hepatic portal vein 76, 77, *77*
hepatocytes 76, *77*
hip 28, *29,* 34
HIV 81
homeostasis 69, 70, 71, 72, 124
Homo sapiens 13, 120, 124
hormonal system 69, 108-109
hormones 67, 72, 108, 112, 114,
    124
humerus *29, 35, 64*
hyoid bone 33
hyperthermia 79
hypothalamus 72, 78, 79, 102,
    103, 104, 109, 124
hypothermia 79

I

ileum *51,* 55
iliac vessels *61*
immune defence system 66, *80,*
    81, 125
immunization *80,* 125
implantation 116
incisor teeth 52-53
infections 80, 81
inferior vena cava *61*
inheritance 14, *14*
inner ear *91,* 92, *93*
insulin 108, *108, 109*
intercostal muscles 58
intestines *23,* 50
involuntary muscle *40,* 41
iris 86-87, *86, 87*
iron 49, 76

J

jaws *29,* 32-33, *33,* 34, *53*
jejunum 55
joints 28, 34-35
joules 48-49, 125
jugular vein *61*

K

keratin 27, *27,* 97, 122
kidney dialysis *71*
kidneys 18, *72, 72, 73,* 74-75, *109*
kidney stones 74
knee *30-31,* 34, *34,* 42
kneecap *30, 31*
Krause *96*

L

lacrimal bone 33, *33*
large intestine 50, *51,* 55
larynx (voicebox) 24, 33, *56,* 95
leg muscles *38*
lens 64, 87, *87,* 88, *89*
leucocytes 66
LH (luteinizing hormone) 112
ligaments *34,* 125
light-sensitive cells 88
lips 44, 50, 53
liver 18, *61, 64,* 70
    digestion 50, *51,* 54-55
    nutrients 76-77, *76, 77*
lumbar vertebrae 28, *100*
lungs 18, *56, 57,* 58-59, *58*
    circulation *61,* 62
lymph 60-61,125
    nodes 18, *23,* 60, *60, 61,* 80
    vessels 55, 60-61,*77*
lymphatic system 60-61
lymphocytes *61,* 66, 80, 81

M

macrophages 66, 80, *81*
mammals 12, 13, *13,* 125
mammary glands 12, *13*
medulla
    brain *103,* 104
    kidney 74, *74, 75, 75*
meiosis 22, 116, 122-123
Meissner's corpuscle *96*
membrane 20, *21,* 125
memory 97, *102,* 105
menstrual cycle 112, 114, 125
metabolism 125
metacarpals (hand bones) *29, 31*
metatarsals (foot bones)*29*
middle ear 90, *90, 91*
milk 12, *13,* 118, 121
mind 102, 104-105
minerals 30, 46, 49, 76, 125
mitochondria 116
mitosis 22, 116, 122
mitral valve *63*
molecules 16-17, 48, 94, *108,* 125
motor centre *102,* 103
mouth 44, 50, *95*
mucus *55, 59,* 94

N

muscle layers *38-39*
muscle tissue 20, 40-41, *40*
muscles 14, 24-25, 42-43, 44-45,
    125
    breathing 58
    digestive tract 50, *55*
    eyeball *86, 87*
    heat 78-79
    heart 62
    skeletal 36-37
    uterus 118
muscular system 18, *18*
myofibres 40-41, 44
myofilaments 40-41, *40, 41*
myosin 40-41, *40, 41*

N

nails 97, *97*
nasal cavity 95, *95*
nephrons 74, 75
nerve cells (neurones) 22, *23,* 89,
    100
nerve fibres 88
nerve impulses 86
nerves *18,* 100-101
    autonomic 106
nerve signals 72,100,*102,*105,*107*
    sensory 88,89,*90,*92,*94,94,96*
nervous system *18,* 99
neural network 99, 100
neutrophils 66
noradrenaline 109
nose 56, 94, *95*
nucleus 21, *21,* 22, 116, 122
nutrients *55,* 76, 125
    absorption 50, *54-55*
    transport 60, 66, 118

O

occipital bone *32, 33*
oesophagus (gullet) 50, 55, *55*
oestrogen 112
olfactory sense 94
optic nerve 87, 88, *89*
orbit (eye socket) 28, *32, 33, 86, 87*
organ of Corti *93*
ossicles (ear bones) 33, *91, 93*
osteocyte (bone cell) 20
osteogenesis 32
ovaries *109,* 112, *113, 117*
oviduct 112, 114, 116
ovulation 112
ovum 20, 112
oxygen 16, 17, 70
    breathing 56, 59
    circulation 66, 118

P

Pacinian corpuscle *96*

P

pancreas 50, *51,* 54, 108, *108, 109*
parasympathetic nerves 107
parathyroid *109*
patella (kneecap) *30, 31*
pelvis (hipbone) 28, *29,* 34
penis 114, *115*
pericardium 62
period 112
periosteum 30
peripheral nervous system 106
peristalsis 50, 125
phalanges (finger or toe bones) *29*
pharynx 50
phosphorus 16, 17, 30
pituitary gland 72, *103, 109,* 112
placenta 118, *119*
plasma 67, 125
platelets 67, 82
pregnancy 111
premolar teeth 52-53
primates 12, *13,* 120, 125
progesterone 112
prostate gland *115*
proteins 16, 26, 40, 122, 125
    digestion 46, 49, 54
puberty 121
pubic bone *113, 119*
pulmonary vessels *57, 61, 63, 57,*
    125
pulse 64, 65, *65*
pupil 86-87, *86, 87*
pyloris *55*

R

radial artery 64, *65*
radius (forearm bone) 28, 42, *83*
rectum 50, 55
red blood cells 20, 22 *23,* 66, *66,*
    67, 81
renal tubule 74, 75
renal vessels *61, 73, 74, 75*
renin *109*
reproductive system 110-111
respiration 56, 59, 125
respiratory system *18,* 56-57
retina 87, *87,* 88, 89, *89*
Rhesus blood group 83
ribs *18,* 28, *29,* 31, 58
rods 88
Ruffini corpuscle *96*

S

sacrum *29*
saliva 50, 53, 94
scapula (shoulder blade) 30
sciatic nerve 100
sclera *86, 87,* 89
scrotum 114, *115*
sebaceous gland 26, *26*

index

acknowledgements

Carlton Books would like to thank: Liz Joseph, Fiona Knowles and Zoë Maggs for design assistance; Jane Parker for the index; Lol Henderson for editorial assistance; Julian Baum and Geoff Fowler for illustrations; Mary Bartolo, Christopher Blake, Candy Day, Emma Eckersley, Heloise Evans, Billy Kebble, Christopher Keightley, Hannah and Joshua Porter, Fiona Marsh, Charlotte and Oliver Monguel, Edward Moody, Thomas New, Lian Ng, Eugenia Olavide Goya, Charlie Quinn, Kelly Richardson, Daniel Sawyer, Kayleigh Swan, and James White for modelling and Karen Testorf at Paul Binhold, Germany. Special thanks go to the staff at ESP and in particular to Jane Seamer, Peter Seamer and Diana Harmer without whom the project would not have succeeded.

The publishers would also like to thank the following sources for their kind permission to reproduce the pictures in this book:

Robert Harding Picture Library; Images Colour Library/Horizon; **Rex Features; Science Photo Library/**Alex Bartel; Professor Marcel Bess; Biology Media; Dr G Oran Bredberg; BSIP, LECA; BSIP VEM; Dr Jeremy Burgess; CNRI; Department of Clinical Radiology, Salisbury District Hospital; A B Dowsett; Professor C Ferlaud/CNRI; Simon Fraser; Adam Hart-Davis; Manfred Kage; Krassorsky/ BSIP; Francis Leroy, Biocosmos; Renee Lynn; David Madison; Will & Deni McIntyre; Eammon McNulty; Professor P Motta, Department of Anatomy, University "La Sapienza", Rome; Professors P Motta,

G Macchiarelli, A Caggiati & F M Magliocca; Professors P Motta, K R Porter & P M Andrew; Larry Mulvehill; Dr Gopal Murti; S Nagendra; Omikron; Alfred Pasieka; D Philips; St Bartholomew's Hospital; Andy Sacks; Secchi/Lecaque/Roussel/CNRI; Stanford Eye Clinic; James Stevenson; Andrew Syred; Geoff Tompkins; **Tony Stone Images; Windrush/**Kevin Carlson; Michael Gore; Gordon Langsbury.

Every effort has been made to acknowledge correctly and contact the source and/or copyright holder of each picture, and Carlton Books Limited apologizes for any unintentional errors or omissions which will be corrected in future editions of this book.